THE UNLIKEABLES

How to step into your individual
leadership power.

Shevonne Joyce

Copyright © 2019 Shevonne Joyce

First published in Australia in 2019 by KMD Press
www.kmdpress.com.au

National Library of Australia
Cataloguing-in-Publication data:

The Unlikeables/ Shevonne Joyce
Non-Fiction – self help Non Fiction – leadership

ISBN 978-0-6486948-5-4 (sc)
ISBN 978-0-6486948-6-1 (e)

Disclaimer

The views and opinions expressed in this book belong solely to the author. They do not reflect the views or opinions of, nor are they shared, supported, or endorsed in any manner by, any other person or organisation. This book in no way constitutes professional advice and should not be relied upon as such. The author is not liable for any damage or negative consequences caused as a result of relying on the information in this book.

Material in this book is accurate and up to date (unless denoted as archived material), and the author does not guarantee and accepts no legal liability whatsoever arising from or connected to, the accuracy, reliability, currency or completeness of any material contained in this book or in any referenced material.

All rights reserved. Content in this book is protected by copyright and all intellectual property belongs to the author. This book and its contents may not be sold, used, published, reproduced, distributed or copied without the author's express permission. All inquiries should be made to the author.

About the author

Shevonne Joyce has built a trusted brand, with her innovative thought leadership reaching over 60 countries and 3.9+ million.

Shevonne is a Brand Strategist who helps clients develop timeless and deeply admired leadership brands, from the inside out. She works with clients who want to become unforgettable and iconic brands; designing their success across business strategy, leadership effectiveness and personal brand. Her unique approach isn't for everyone, but for those who are up for a total mindset rewire, the results are compelling.

Shevonne is also the co-owner of a global, luxury children's fashion brand, stella.phoenix, alongside her husband, Paul. Stella, as Shevonne affectionately calls it, designs timeless pieces that enable children to experience the magic and enchantment of childhood through what they wear. The brand, at its heart, is about celebrating the expression of individual identity. Stella has been invited and accepted into international fashion shows and has a devoted customer base and following.

Shevonne has been appointed as a judge for both the Telstra Business Awards and the Women's Business Awards, has been named as one of the Top 10 Australian Women Entrepreneurs by My Entrepreneur magazine, one of the Top Business Thinkers by Smartcompany.com.au, alongside Naomi Simson, in the 99 'Limit Breaking' Female Founders by Thrive, and has been nominated in the AFR Top 100 Women of Influence Awards.

Dedication

*To Stevii and Lenny,
Shine bright.*

*Love you always,
Mumma x*

BOOK TEAM

Lead Researcher: Chrys Stevenson

Photography: Jo Westaway, Jo Westaway Photography

Legals: Marianne Marchesi, Legalite

Cover Design & Layout: Jennifer Dinsdale, Clarke Street Creative

Publisher: Karen McDermott, KMD Press

CONTENTS

Foreword by Ginger Gorman — 1

Chapter One - The Problem is the Answer — 3
Chapter Two - Finding Likeable in Unlikeable — 15
Chapter Three - Who We Are and What We Do — 27
Chapter Four - The Brand Promise — 39
Chapter Five - The False Equivalency — 49
Chapter Six - The Gender Penalty — 59
Chapter Seven - Grappling with a Unique Mind — 73
Chapter Eight - Re-Birth — 83
Chapter Nine - Shedding the 'Shoulds' — 95
Chapter Ten - The Grand Slam of Unlikeability — 109
Chapter Eleven - The Link — 121
Chapter Twelve - Becoming an Icon — 133

Final Word and Thank you — 144
Endnotes — 147
Bibliography — 156

FOREWORD
by Ginger Gorman

As a freelance journalist and non-fiction author, it sometimes feels that being unlikeable is the cost of doing business. After all, my job involves finding out things people don't want me to know and telling the public things they don't want to hear. It's not a profession for the faint-hearted.

On the other hand, journalism is a business like any other. It's how I earn my living. If people don't like me and my stories, I can't do mundane things like pay the mortgage and the school fees. Like many self-employed women, sometimes I feel I'm walking a tightrope between the need to be both likeable and unlikeable. If I'm unlikeable, people won't buy my work. If I try not to upset people, my stories will end up shallow and boring with the same result - people won't buy my work. Is it a Catch-22? Is the only possible outcome unpopularity and poverty?

This book is about these kinds of dilemmas. How do we reconcile the natural desire, and the economic need, to be liked, when claiming the freedom to be ourselves, being innovative, and making hard, but necessary, business decisions so often rubs people up the wrong way?

Shevonne Joyce has tackled these issues head-on in her book. Bravely taking us on her own journey, Shevonne offers up her own 'unlikeability' as a specimen, putting it under the microscope and examining it from every angle. What Shevonne discovers is astounding and will change the way you think about being unlikeable.

In Chapter 9, Shevonne writes about Sudanese-Australian, Yassmin Abdel-Magied. Yassmin was viciously attacked after making a fairly innocuous comment about ANZAC Day in 2017. There's no doubt Yassmin was the victim of intersectional discrimination. She was reviled for the 'sin' of being an outspoken woman, a woman of colour, and a Muslim. Shevonne shows how Yassmin took the torrent of hate that drove her out of the country and used it to create a global platform to spread her message about racism and the need for tolerance and diversity.

While my only 'sin' is being female, I faced much the same experience in 2013 after news broke about two 'doting dads' who had just been arrested as paedophiles. I'd featured them some years earlier in a 'feel-good' story about same-sex couples. Neither I, nor anyone else, had any idea of their crimes at the time I recorded the interview. I didn't approach the story as an investigative journalist - I was a morning radio broadcaster. I had just done my job. Now, years later, I was suddenly Public Enemy No. 1, branded as a paedophile-lover, and the recipient of a stream of the foulest, most violent, distressing online abuse you can imagine. It was like being skinned alive.

Mine is an extreme example. However, as Shevonne so brilliantly explains in her book, when being yourself, or doing your job, makes you unlikeable, you can let it defeat you, change you, send you scurrying back inside your shell, or, you can use all that negative energy as rocket fuel. Like Yassmin, I chose the latter. I used that dreadful experience to get to know the predator trolls who attacked me and threatened my family. I developed an innovative method of research I call 'radical empathy' to infiltrate their world and understand their motives. And then, struggling freelance journalist that I was, I wrote a book that's become a best-seller, that's influencing how governments and police respond to cyber-hate, and which has created international opportunities for me to shed light on a dark and sinister underworld that very few understand.

As Shevonne suggests in this book, I claimed my 'unlikeability', gathered up all that hate, and turned it into a chance to change the world.

And, with Shevonne's help, you can too.

Ginger Gorman

CHAPTER ONE

The Problem is the Answer

Why do human beings find the idea of being 'unlikeable' so terrifying?

Because it cuts to the heart of our deepest fears.

Was it hard to pick up this book? Did you cautiously thumb through the pages, wondering what this unlikeable caper was all about? Was there a moment of resistance, of challenge, before you took the plunge and brought it home with you?

SIDE NOTE: Super glad you did.

You see, we like to pride ourselves as quite advanced beings. When we look at advancements in science, technology and humanity, in a lot of ways that's true. At our core, we continue to have primal drivers and needs that are key for our survival, including feeling loved and accepted. Many of us, therefore, fear rejection. This is the basis of why we have such a difficult time with the concept of unlikeability.

I'm not going to lie; writing this book has been extraordinary and challenging. Extraordinary in the sense that it changed how I saw the world, myself and others. (It would be great to hear what you take from it!) Challenging in that truly understanding the human mind is far more complex than I could ever have imagined. There are many ideas out in the world about human behaviour, and how we think and exist. Some of them are, frankly, completely unfounded. Others are hotly contested, even amongst experts. Other ideas, well, we have the best understanding we can, but there's still much to learn. Scientific knowledge is continually evolving.

In researching this book I've looked at neuroscience, psychology, business, branding, anecdotes, opinions, as well as a philosophical view on likeability. I'm not a neuroscientist, a psychologist, or a philosopher. What I share in this book relates to my personal journey and discovery within the context of understanding my own unlikeability. It's shared to help you on your expedition, but it's not a complete source of information. Instead, it's a contribution to a larger discussion and should be considered as such.

When I began this journey, I didn't anticipate that it would turn out the way it has. As you'll see, I was looking for something else. I was looking for an answer, any answer, aside from being unlikeable. In fact, unlikeability was supposed to be the problem I set out to solve, not the answer. The deeper I went, the more I learnt, the more the dawning realisation crept up, like a sunrise you are trying to avoid because you have to get up for work and you barely slept a wink last night. Know the feeling?

Trekking this path required me to face the deepest of fears, bust the strongest of assumptions, unzip my insides, turn myself over, and shake me all out - like you do to a handbag when you can't find your credit card. Yes, there have been moments where I've had to challenge my own thinking. That is, as I like to put it, clear my own bullshit. Like any journey of self-discovery, it's been like mining for diamonds and has involved a lot of digging. At times it has been dark, damp, uncomfortable and a bit messy, but each diamond I've uncovered and polished has been worth it. There's so much I've learnt about myself, but a key lesson has been to see conflict and discomfort in a new light. Once upon a time, when a resistance or objection would come up, I'd have to do something with it. Imagine juggling the thing like a hot potato, while jogging around trying to figure out where to put it. That was me. What I've learnt is that sometimes we know what to do with it, and other times it's okay to take time to honour the digestion process.

In fact, there are still parts of this book that I'll be digesting long after it's published.

What you take from this will depend on where you are in your journey. There's what I have to offer you, and what you have to offer yourself. While I can provide eggs, flour, milk, sugar, and yeast for dough, you bring the fillings, flavours and toppings. This journey is uniquely yours, and what you have to offer is uniquely yours. Your formula for success is uniquely yours. This, therefore, is not a 'standard formula.' As we move through each chapter, think about how it might apply to you, or what else you have to complement what's being said. Reading and learning is valuable, however the learning that we experience while implementing new knowledge is truly the icing on the cake.

What was it like deciding to write about being unlikeable?

Well. Brené Brown, a research professor at the University of Houston and #1 New York Times best-selling author and speaker, recalled in her Netflix special, The Call to Courage, that her husband freaked out when she said she had decided to do a Ted Talk on vulnerability.[1] When I realised I was going to write about being unlikeable there was a similar moment of WTF. Who writes a book on being unlikeable?

"This is a huge risk," I thought, imagining my whole soul laid bare for everyone to feast on. And then, with a steely resolve, I decided I was destined to write about it anyway.

There have been various responses to this idea, ranging from, "This is the most fascinating thing I've ever heard!" to "Huh?" My Dad lovingly said he always knew I had a book in me, "but never thought it would be about this." That made me laugh. To be fair, there's many adventures I've ended up on over the years that have left my Dad scratching his head.

The truth is I love all of the feedback, because it shows that this topic has got the cogs turning in people's minds and it's pushing the boundaries of thinking. This book could be a wild success, or it could be an epic fail. Regardless, I've put my all into it and I'm proud of it.

How do you know this book is for you?

This book is for you if:

- You've ever been called unlikeable, or told you need to change part of who you inherently are, in order to achieve success.
- You're the oddball in your field and want to explore how that could be the fuel to your success.
- People-pleasing is consuming your life and work like a hungry caterpillar.
- You've ever been ridiculed or struggled to find your place in the world. Rest assured; you're in the right place here and now.
- It's also for you if you are terrified of standing out from the crowd.
- Last, but not least, it's for those who are open and willing to challenge themselves and grow.

Some of us will have a direct experience of being labelled "unlikeable." For others the fear of potentially being unlikeable is enough to strike terror. In fact, some people who picked up this book will have put it down and moved on to the next one for that very reason; it scared them and they're not ready. That's okay, they'll come back when they are.

It's important to care about how we impact others and to strive to help shape the world in a positive way for the greater good. However, some of us will spend a lot of unnecessary time and emotional labour agonising over how we're perceived. In the process, we can lose ourselves.

Understanding what causes a person to be likeable or unlikeable to another requires us to look at what the experts tell us about how our brain processes information.

I recall the day when a mentor of mine told me that the reaction I was having to another person was, in fact, a reflection of what I was rejecting within myself.

I thought this idea was preposterous.

"But I am not like them!" I protested.

"They are reflecting something that is within you," he said, patiently. "We can't see in others what isn't within ourselves."

He asked me to sit with it, and simply be open to the idea. So I did.

This conversation activated a part of me that had been, somewhat, in hibernation, snuggled deep beneath the surface of my being for years on end, breathing deeply, still living, being, growing and feeling, but not active. This is the moment when a light switch flicked on within me and illuminated a deep fascination for what really happens beneath the surface of likeability. Just like that, the bear woke up and peeked his nose out of the cave as the sun thawed the ice. After a keen sniff, the bear went on the hunt.

You see, unlikeability is something I have struggled with my entire life. I remember my very first experience with it. I was 5 or 6 years old - in prep. My report card came home and on it my prep teacher had written that I was "bossy." A specific example of this behaviour was that after play time, all the kids were supposed to line up and wait for the teacher outside our classroom. Me, being me, organised them all and got everyone all lined up. In my 5-6-year-old mind, I was being helpful because I didn't want them to get in trouble for not doing what was asked. To me, I was being caring. "Bossy" was a shock. When I think back to this moment now, I laugh. I love the little girl I was so fiercely. But back then? 5-6-year-old me? I was crushed. I cried. My Dad, quite amused at the whole situation, told me not to worry about it; I was perfect the way I was. Of course, at the time, I didn't believe him. He was my Dad. He was supposed to think that!

I didn't realise that my experience was a hint about who I was meant to be. That my leadership skills, thoughtfulness and care were, in fact, strengths.

As I grew up and moved through my personal and professional life, I continued to receive feedback about my strong-minded, outspoken, results-oriented, take-charge, big, visionary personality. I tried to temper myself accordingly. Of course, we all have development points and I'm no exception to that. There have been many mentors, managers and influencers in my life who saw the value in my potential and cared enough to expertly steer me in the right direction - my Dad included.

I remember one of the best bosses I've ever had, from the early days of my professional career. At my farewell on the last day I worked for him, he fondly recalled the time I walked into his office and told him a decision he had made was, as I put it, "Shit."

I cringe thinking about it now (not my finest moment!) and definitely don't recommend this course of action in a professional setting. If I could live my time over again, I would have been more tactful and polite about delivering my perspective. But at the time he laughed and said:

"No one has ever had the courage to say that to me before, and it was because you cared."

Indeed.

Along the way, well-meaning colleagues and business peers gave me advice. Their advice was always from a place of care, but always pointed to me changing the essence of who I am. For example, one person said to me:

"Maybe you should be less 'no BS.'"

Each time this would happen, I'd listen dutifully, and I'd try to take it on board. I tried to contain myself, in order to be worthy of approval. Like an eager traveller trying to stuff too many belongings into a suitcase, I kept trying to stuff myself into an 'acceptable woman' box. I piled my insides into that box, and sat on the lid, while bits and pieces burst out the sides. I tried to be who others wanted and needed me to be in different life situations, but it was impossible to maintain. Eventually I realised I couldn't stem the flow of who I truly was. It was excruciating trying to pretend I was someone I wasn't, and deeply unfulfilling and lonely trying to convince others that I was worthy; both personally and professionally. Each failed attempt to change left me feeling like I was an apple, rotten at the core; that something was fundamentally wrong with me. It was largely a silent struggle on the inside while I tried on different suits like some kind of confused chameleon.

What happens when we're in the grip of constantly analysing our interactions with others?

We begin to base our success on the success metrics of others. We lose our own voice. We forget what we think. We spend so much time and energy trying to anticipate and cater for every possible eventuality that we lose our sense of agency. We get to a point where we ask ourselves, "Who the hell am I?"

This is why we need to grapple with our fear of unlikeability. This is an example of what leaders who suffer from excruciating people-pleasing go through. It can have serious consequences - personally and professionally. Feeling constrained by your fear of unlikeability is amplified when you put yourself on a public platform, especially if you're disrupting or agitating for change.

I'm not demonising people-pleasing. We all like to please people. We all aim to do it in varying degrees. But it's who we're pleasing and the lengths we go to in the process that determines our relationship with the compulsion to please. And it's how that ultimately impacts our outcomes that matters.

Dejected, and unable to shake off the unlikeability, I tried to carry on, undeterred. But it was there with me all the time, like a ball and chain that I dragged around, hoping one day I'd find the bolt-cutters to set myself free. When I met new people, the fear and self-doubt loomed.

One woman at a business networking event randomly started talking to me about how likeability was a key issue with branding for some women. She rounded off her comments with: "I don't buy from women I don't like."

I remember looking at her looking at me and wondering what was the point of this conversation. Was she asking my opinion? Was she trying to tell me something? There were other people standing there, but she was looking at me. Heart thumping, I looked the other way and glossed over the conversation, but it was the straw that broke the camel's back. It wasn't the first time this issue had come up, and it wouldn't be the last. The ball and chain had fractured the leg of my pride. I decided I had to solve my likeability problem. It was a problem I couldn't put aside any longer.

But as hard as I tried, nothing worked. People told me to forget about it, but I couldn't. The secret algorithm to likeability outwitted me relentlessly. It became a self-fulfilling prophecy; I thought I was unlikeable, so that's how people reacted to me. I continued to have interactions and experiences where I got the impression that people didn't find me particularly palatable. After years in the boxing ring with my nemesis, Unlikeability, I finally called a time out. We stepped out of the ring. We took our gloves off. We unwrapped our bloodied knuckles and slumped onto the bench, with sweat pouring from our glands. I decided to review my progress. Pretending to be someone I wasn't didn't work, and I couldn't go on with this interminable battle against myself. What was left?

Then, it hit me like a bolt from the blue.

I'd looked over, under and around it. The only option left was to face the painful reality I had been trying to avoid; I was different, and unlikeable.

I stepped into my unlikeability for the first time and I sat with it. I fully immersed myself in it and opened myself up to what it was here to teach me. First port of call, I needed to understand why I was unlikeable. What is it that determines whether we're likeable or unlikeable to others? What happens within our brain? I thought maybe if I could understand that, I would learn how to not be that. Diving into the research was a big moment. In my mind I imagined the 'this is it' scenario as if, at any second, there was going to be a rabbit out of a hat: "Ta-da! Here's why you're so unlikeable and here's what you need to change."

Well. There was a rabbit out of a hat experience. In fact, there were several, and you'll come across them throughout this book. Let's start with the first big question: What is it that makes us likeable and unlikeable to others?

Note: At the end of each chapter you will find tasks for you to do (like the one on the next page) and space to write notes and reflections.

TASK: Be open to the idea that unlikeability might not be what it seems on the surface.

How has unlikeability impacted you to date? What would you like to achieve at the end of this book?

CHAPTER TWO

◇◇

Finding Likeable in Unlikeable

How true is the suggestion that how we respond to other people is a clue to how we feel about ourselves?

Turns out my mentor was onto something (and I know he is reading this, so: *Thank you for your wisdom*). It all relates back to a process called 'projection.' You've probably heard people say in passing, "They are just projecting onto you."

Where did the concept of projection come from?

Projection can be traced back to ancient history. The Babylonian Talmud (500 AD) warns:

"Do not taunt your neighbour with the blemish you yourself have."[2]

We've all heard of the saying about glass houses and throwing stones, right?

Psychoanalyst Anna Freud put forward the idea that projection is the way we deal with thoughts, motivations, desires or feelings that we can't accept as our own.[3] So, we process them by putting them outside of ourselves and attributing them to someone else. Carl Jung considered that the 'unacceptable' parts of our personality are easier to see in others than ourselves. He called this the 'shadow archetype', the dark part, or the part we don't want to know about ourselves and that we wish wasn't there.[4]

In the 1800s Ludwig Feuerbach, an 'enlightenment thinker,' employed projection to critique religion, claiming that God is a reflection of ourselves.[5]

Deepak Chopra discussed projection in our personal relationships:

"However good or bad you feel about your relationship right now, the person you are with at this moment is the right person, because he or she is the mirror of who you are inside... When you struggle with your partner you are struggling with yourself – every fault you see in them touches a denied weakness in yourself."[6]

German novelist and poet Hermann Hesse suggested that, in line with our fear of being rejected, we have a fear of not being 'good' which causes us to project 'badness' onto others. He said:

"If you hate a person, you hate something in him that is part of yourself. What isn't part of ourselves doesn't disturb us."[7]

Firstly, hate is a strong word to describe feelings about others or ourselves. I hope there's no one out there who would go so far as to say they 'hate' me! Nonetheless, I thought about how this might apply to a couple of socially undesirable traits, like selfishness and greed. If I recoil at these characteristics in others, could they be part of me?

I noticed myself switching into 'reconcile' mode as I worked through it all.

"I consider myself to be a thoughtful and generous person," I reasoned. "I'm morally opposed to selfishness and greed. I conscientiously strive every day to serve others and be kind. Despite this, is it possible that I could be capable of these characteristics, given the right conditions? EVEN IF I choose not to act on them?"

Could it be possible that those undesirable traits are in there somewhere, lying dormant, and my reaction to them is my rejection of them? Could it be that they remind me of an unpleasant interaction with someone else whose selfishness or greed had an impact on me?

I remembered a client who experienced something similar. She called with a staff performance issue and asked an insightful and brilliant question, "Is the problem her, or is it me?"

When we discussed the situation in detail, it occurred to the client that the staff member reminded her of her mother.

Curiously, I asked, "What part of both of them do you see in yourself?"

"My need to have control," she responded. "I'm really glad this came up."

The idea that our reactions to others could teach us something about ourselves is intriguing.

Moving on to what we like about each other, the research suggests the process is the same. When we see qualities within another person that align with us, we idolise them.

"It's like 'falling in love' with ourselves," my researcher noted. "A form of projected narcissism, if you will!"

"How weird, but cool!" I thought.

I turned my attention to some of my best clients. What would they say about some of the criticism I have received?

"They said I'm money-hungry because I'm passionate about building a profitable business," I said.

The client responded, "But you are so generous! How can they possibly think that?"

Upon discussing my unlikeability, another client said, "I understand that you're broadly unlikeable because you're bucking trends, but I personally can't see how someone wouldn't like you."

Another, "How could they have thought you're intimidating? When I first saw you, I thought, 'I want to work with a powerful woman like that.' I found it inspiring."

Now, this was by no means a scientific survey, but I found the difference in observations between my best clients and others quite interesting. I realised that two different people could see the same subject and draw polar-opposite conclusions about them. One person saw a woman who was intimidating. The other saw an inner power that so inspired them, they wanted to step within its orbit. At the time their conclusions were drawn, neither knew any more about me than the other.

Thinking back to the previous example about selfishness and greed, how do we know our perceptions are accurate? For example, what if I perceive someone to be greedy, but it's not greed at all? What if, with the information I have, it seems to be greed but there's information that I'm not privy to which could change that conclusion?

It was here I began thinking about our individual reality and perceptions, which, of course, is extremely complicated. My research led me to neuroscientist David Eagleman.

In a Ted Talk, Eagleman made some interesting points about different perceptions of the same reality.[8] For example, he says our perception of reality is the 'complete' one to us, but there are parts of reality - such as the full spectrum of light, or a dog's sense of smell - that we can't experience. He mentioned that if we could talk to the dog, it would likely be surprised to learn we can't smell the same scent on the ground that it can.

"Wow!" I thought and did some more searching on David Eagleman. In an interview on the Art of Charm Podcast, he discussed our reality further, saying:

"Everybody essentially is living on their own planet."[9]

He went on to say that while we may be looking at the same object, different people will perceive the object according to their own individual knowledge and experience.

Similarly, neuroscientist Anil Seth did a Ted Talk, in which he said our perception of the world is simply a "hallucination" based on how our brain organises information.[10] We gather information based on factors like our experience, personality, culture, beliefs, genetics, etc.

When we apply this to branding or leadership, it translates to either a meeting, or clashing, of the minds. Yes, we look for clues and signposts in our assessments, based on shared social understanding. But unless we are aware of and open to the idea that there could be more than our own realm of understanding, could all roads lead back to conclusions based on our own preconceptions and prejudices? Instead of a genuine quest for knowledge, are we just setting out to prove ourselves right?

I felt something shift within me. Suddenly everything I ever thought I knew had been challenged - in a good way. I started to wonder if I was unlikeable at all, or whether I was focusing too much on the criticisms I'd received, instead of the compliments.

What if all the things that I thought were my weaknesses, were, in fact, strengths?

I delved into The Courage to be Disliked by Ichiro Kishimi and Fumitake Koga.[11] This book tells the story of conversations between a philosopher and his student about how to achieve happiness.

The philosopher points out to the student:

"You notice only your shortcomings because you've resolved to not start liking yourself. In order to not like yourself, you don't see your strong points, and focus only on your shortcomings."[12]

This brought up confronting questions for me. Was my focus on how unlikeable I was amplified because, underneath it all, I didn't like myself?

The truth is, before I embarked on learning about unlikeability, I didn't like myself. I didn't hate myself. I had sort of resigned myself to the fact that this is who I am. Like, "This is my lot in life, so I'd better make the most of it and get on as best as I can." Even though I tried to deny it to myself, I knew, deep down, that being unlikeable had become part of my identity. But now, I was seeing that being unlikeable and not liking myself were related. Did I want to continue not liking myself? Hell, no. But did I want to keep being unlikeable? Well… Wait, what?! That unnerving pause for deliberation rocked my foundations like an earthquake… Did I want to be unlikeable? Who in their right mind would want to be unlikeable?!

I spent some time pondering the possibility that I didn't want to let go of being unlikeable and that, maybe, just maybe, this had hindered my progress on this mission. What did I get out of it? Well, to me the other option was becoming a sheep - living a life I ultimately didn't want, to please and appease others. Being unlikeable gave me creative freedom. Being likeable meant losing control. I imagine that people-pleasers feel a similar loss of control at the idea of rocking the boat. Yet, the weirdest thing was occurring to me. Likeability and unlikeability weren't as separate as I initially thought. My clients thought I was likeable even though I was unlikeable. Unlikeability = likeability and likeability = unlikeability, too. What does that mean exactly?

I drew a Venn diagram.

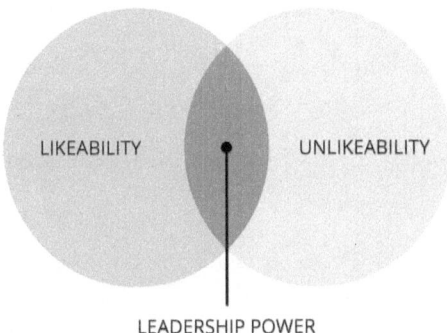

In order to find our true leadership power, we have to understand and embrace our **whole self.**

If I try to be unlikeable, I'll stray from my innate self. If I try to be likeable, the same problem will occur. The value is in the fusion between the two. In other words, our true likeability sits within our unlikeability. That is, when we understand what our real strengths are, and not just the ones people tell us we should have, we live those strengths. Living our strengths makes us likeable to the right people. For example, what I've noticed when I spend time with my clients is how effortless it is. They get me. They respect me. We enjoy working together. We challenge each other in an empowered way. When I'm with those who dislike me, my soul feels crushed. My shine tarnishes. I become a shell of Shevonne.

I recalled a conversation that I had with a woman in my network about this topic. She told me that she's naturally a bubbly kind of person, but she had to, essentially, kill that part of herself because people gave her feedback that she seemed like a "bimbo"; that she should change in order to be taken more seriously. In response she tried to pop her bubbles. She said:

"I began to notice my bubbliness every time it appeared and squashed it down."

What people were telling her was, they didn't like her bubbly nature and as we've discussed, that could be for a myriad of reasons related to what it brought up for them. But this unlikeable part of herself is part of her genius. It's likeable to other people! When we listen to these judgements, we become isolated and lonely - surrounded by people who continually reinforce that we're not good enough.

Embracing unlikeability is, therefore, about belonging. Who ever thought we'd put unlikeability and belonging in the same sentence?!

In her Netflix special, Brené Brown defines belonging as:

"... the opposite of fitting in."

She says:

"True belonging doesn't require us to change who we are; it requires us to be who we are."[13]

Rather than trying to find **where** we belong, it's **how** we belong. When we belong in the way we were always meant to, we align with others who are also on that frequency. When we try to find a place to belong, we try to conform to the requirements of that space, instead of defining our own. We cannot define how we belong without embracing our unlikeability.

Powerful.

Before we move on, let's define what embracing our 'unlikeability' means in the context of this book. It's not a pass to be mean-spirited, to harm others, or to act however we like without consequence. That (as my Dad so poetically puts it) is the definition of "arsehole-ism."

There's a difference between finding someone inherently unlikeable and being genuinely and legitimately concerned (or horrified) by their actions (or inactions).

The idea that positively embracing our unlikeability and being kind can't go hand in hand is a myth. They must go hand in hand for the two sections of the Venn diagram to meld together. In fact, as I've discovered, embracing our unlikeability can be the kindest thing we do for ourselves, our clients, our market, and the world. You'll understand more about why by the time you finish this book.

On the whole, we must acknowledge that being leaders in our field means we are shaping and influencing those we lead: having a powerful and positive impact on other human beings. It's a responsibility that must be taken seriously and treated with care. Quite rightly we have legal obligations, but also moral and ethical ones.

Embracing our unlikeability is about:

- Individual empowerment
- Inner power
- Redefining beauty and worth
- Responsibility
- Reflection and awareness
- Deconstructing systems of inequality
- Tapping into our unique genius
- Reinvention
- Freedom

All of this will become clearer as you move through each chapter of this book and learn what feeds the beast of unlikeability.

TASK: Next time you experience being rejected, or find yourself rejecting someone else, stop and ask yourself, *"What might be contributing to these feelings?"*

Honestly reflect within yourself, "What could this person be bringing up for me? What could I be bringing up for them?"

_____
_____
_____
_____
_____
_____
_____
_____
_____
_____
_____
_____
_____
_____

CHAPTER THREE

Who We Are and What We Do

To what extent does who we are shape what we do and achieve?

Lots of business advice suggests that all we need are certain strategies, formulas and skills to change outcomes. That's not to say there aren't ways to go about building your success that are more attuned to results than others, but I'd be doing you a disservice if I was an absolutist about the efficacy of blanket leadership strategies. Who we are influences outcomes.

How?

Let's start with personality.

Our personality is the result of genetics, upbringing and life experience. There are common personality traits but even these vary in degree from person to person. For example: how open a person is to new experiences and ways of thinking, how agreeable they are, and their levels of neuroticism, perfectionism, introversion or extroversion. What's interesting is the way different traits can be viewed as beneficial or detrimental, depending on who you are and who is perceiving those characteristics. As we'll cover in the upcoming chapters, this can depend on personal attributes, including, but not limited to race, gender, sexuality, religion and disability. It also depends on our level of privilege or disadvantage within the social system we live in.

I want to be clear that I'm not purporting to represent all groups, especially the ones I don't belong to, by writing this book. I hope this book will help people to reflect on the inequalities we perpetuate, whether consciously or not. In exploring unlikeability and the barriers it creates for people, we have to face some confronting realities - the kind that many don't want to face. But by choosing not to confront this topic, we hold society back as a whole. For example, despite the insistence that we live in a meritocracy, being a white male remains the most advantageous attribute for a leader in a country like Australia.

If we have a choice not to recognise privilege, or, if we can't see it, that's evidence of our privilege. Privilege comes in many forms. Take for example, white privilege.

Anti-racism activist Peggy McIntosh, who is also a speaker, scholar, feminist, and senior research associate of the Wellesley Centers for Women, describes 'white privilege' as follows:

"I have come to see white privilege as an invisible package of unearned assets that I can count on cashing in each day, but about which I was 'meant' to remain oblivious. White privilege is like an invisible weightless knapsack of special provisions, maps, passports, codebooks, visas, clothes, tools, and blank checks."[14]

Or, male privilege.

In her speech at the 2017 CEDA Women in Leadership conference, journalist and women's rights activist Tracey Spicer gave the analogy of an aquarium that's set up perfectly to accommodate the needs of tropical fish. She said:

"Think of men as a school of tropical fish and their organisation's corporate culture as the aquarium in which they swim. As long as the aquarium's set up to accommodate their needs, the tropical fish will thrive. While their tummies are full, their gills are moving in and out and their little tails are swishing, they won't give a moment's thought to the ecosystem in which they live.

Speaking generally, I think this is how men experience corporate culture. As long as it sustains them, they barely notice it's there. If a woman has difficulty surviving within that culture, they're seen as failing to adapt - of not being a good corporate 'fit'. When they leave, it's because they 'just couldn't hack it.'"

Tracey continued:

"What if, in a rush of blood to the head, our fish-fancier decides to add some diversity by throwing a handful of goldfish into his tank of tropical fish? He may have very best of intentions. But if he takes no account of what goldfish need to survive, his attempt at diversification will fail.

Before long, the goldfish will start rising to the top... and not in a good way. As long as the environment - the culture of that tank - is only set up for the tropical fish, the goldfish just aren't going to thrive.

The failure to achieve diversity in an ecosystem that's fine-tuned for only one type of fish has nothing to do with the quality or the number of goldfish. You can stuff the aquarium full of the fanciest fantails, and the result will be the same. Gasping for air, they'll swim towards the top, reach the glass ceiling and just peg out. I think most of us know how it feels to be totally exhausted from trying to exist in an environment that takes no account of our particular needs.

Yes. It's possible the odd, hardy goldfish will survive; but it will never be sufficient to maintain equal representation in the tank."[15]

The same analogy fits across privilege more broadly. When an environment is set up perfectly to meet our needs, we don't consider the barriers that exist for others. We assume the problem is theirs, rather than the environment itself. We assume our needs are all the same. We're blind to the inequality. It's the mindset of: *What do they mean, everyone doesn't have equal opportunity to thrive? But we do. Look at us all here, we've all achieved success!*

The reality is, while we may have worked hard, and we may be talented, we're also working in a system that has cleared a path up the ladder for people like us; but not all people.

Here's an example to illustrate. A client of mine who was born in Saudi Arabia, but migrated to Australia with an Arabic surname, confided in me about the struggles she has faced.

When she married her husband, who has an Italian background, upon changing her name she immediately noticed a difference in the way she was received, approached, and the doors that opened for her. She didn't change - her opportunities did. Suddenly, the 'fish in the tank' saw her more as one of them. It was at that point she realised, for the first time, the invisible barriers imposed on her as an Arabic woman; barriers she didn't even notice until they came down. She's one of the most fabulous and talented women I've ever had the pleasure to work with; such a high calibre leader with so much potential who had been held back because of who she is.

Her story is not unusual - there have been studies that demonstrate a name on a resumé can either increase or decrease your chances of gaining a job interview.[16] To some, a name might seem frivolous, but a name is far more than the letters it's made up of. A name is who we are, it's where we've come from, it's our family, our bloodline, our life, who we love, our very being. It represents us. But sometimes being 'us' sets us apart from 'them'.

As another example, James St James, who underwent a female to male transition, experienced something similar. Following his transition, he observed with fascination:

"... how other people were responding to me. In short, I was being treated better by everyday America because people were reading me as a young, white, straight (?!) male. And I recognized many new privileges that came my way because of it... Now that I'm a short white guy, people automatically peg me for a comedian and laugh at the bulk of my mouth zings... I'm still amazed at the amount of people that now immediately shut their mouths the second I open mine. Believe me, my ideas haven't improved at all. I've even tried to derail serious conversations with ludicrous stuff, just to see what would happen – and I'd still be regarded highly."[17]

He also noticed that, as a man:

- he is rarely interrupted
- he gets paid more than he did when he was identified as a woman
- finding work is easier
- he is criticised/reprimanded less
- he can walk home alone and feel safe
- people care about the work he does, not how he looks
- older men are keen to mentor him professionally

- he isn't subjected to 'casual sexism' – e.g. people don't ask him to make them a coffee or decorate or clean up workspaces
- he is given credit for his own success - nobody assumes he had outside help or gained a job or promotion for any reason other than his own talent and hard work by default
- even when he deliberately says stupid things, people just assume he's right

A friend of mine related a similar experience to James St James when she was transitioning from a male to a female. While James had gained male privileges, my friend lost them and experienced gender-based prejudice for the first time.

When he was Leader of the Opposition, Bill Shorten cited a startling example of how being born into a disadvantaged group can dramatically effect your life's trajectory. He said:

"A young Aboriginal man of 18 in Australia is more likely to end up in jail than university."[18]

The claim checked out. ABC's 'Fact Check' determined that:

"... the most recent available data shows a greater proportion of Indigenous men had been to jail in the five years to 2008 than had a bachelor's degree or above in 2011, and a greater proportion were in jail than at university in 2014... The data shows that about 6 percent of Indigenous adult men had been released from prison in the five years to 2008, and 4 per cent were in prison in 2014. When it comes to university attendance, about 4 per cent of Indigenous men reported in 2011 having completed a bachelor's degree or higher, and 2.4 per cent attended university in 2014."[19]

2018 figures from the Australian Bureau of Statistics show that the most economically disadvantaged areas in Australia are, overwhelmingly, those with large Aboriginal populations.[20]

A common argument by many with privilege is the notion that we all have personal responsibility for our choices. Australia likes to consider itself as the land of the 'fair go.' What this fails to take into account is that the options, or choices, available to us differ depending on who we are and the resources we have in the tank. Our opportunity to 'have a crack' is not equal - whether people with privilege see it or not. How heartbreaking, mind blowing, and utter bullshit is that?

How can privileged groups help dismantle the system of inequality? I asked a business acquaintance, who is a woman of colour. While she acknowledged that the answers are complicated, she said that, in her view:

"The first step is for people with privilege to stop denying that the roadblocks exist for disadvantaged groups and [stop] minimising them. Just because you can't see them or don't personally experience them doesn't mean they aren't there. The fact that you can't see them is an example of privilege. The minimising of issues is utterly exhausting and having to constantly justify your experiences to others is degrading."

Here we have an opportunity to reflect within and make conscious decisions about how we participate in the system. Do we want to break the stigmas and barriers that create these inequalities, or maintain them?

This may be an uncomfortable question for those of us with privilege. To be honest, at times I've marinated in shame over my privilege because, like people from other privileged groups, I've benefited from the system without realising it. I recognise that the shame is mine to acknowledge and work through. I've come to a point where I've accepted that I cannot change what has happened, but I can contribute to changing the future by recognising my privilege, being prepared to challenge it, asking questions, listening deeply, and utilising my social advantage to make choices that help uplift others.

What's also interesting about likeability is that people can dislike us, yet still approve of what we do. Similarly, they can disapprove of what we do, and still like us. We'll hear this when they say, "I don't like her, but I respect what she does" or "I know he did something bad, but he is such a nice guy." In these circumstances we're trying to make sense of a person alongside their actions. As we've explored, our perceptions can be influenced by our bias or prejudice. It can also be that the person's actions are contrary to our personal experience of them. We've seen this with celebrities who have intentionally built a certain public persona, only to have their 'other side' exposed. People can exercise a level of choice over their likeability as well - we all do it to varying degrees, depending on what role we're playing and the situation we find ourselves in.

The most fascinating story I've heard about this was that of a famous World War II singer who was revered for being lovely and charming. A client told me about seeing a documentary which disclosed how she managed her brand of being a 'sweetheart.' It was explained that she'd send her husband into venues before her gigs to fix everything and make sure it was perfect. Afterwards, she'd swan in, full of compliments and 'thank you's'. From my client's description it sounded like this woman effectively outsourced her unlikeability to her husband - which meant she never had to be disagreeable.

"Why should a person have to outsource part of their personality to their husband to be considered acceptable?" I thought. Nonetheless, it's an interesting example of the strategies people have used to manage the issues related to unlikeability.

When considering our own unlikeability, or that of others, it's important to work out which parts need work (developing skills, strategies or approaches) and which require a change of perception. If we're asking a group of people to behave differently based on who they are (for example, a person of colour) that's inequality and discrimination. If we participate in it, we are complicit in it. There's no 'but' about it.

I've tried to choose a diverse pool of leaders to write about in this book but, at the end of the day, it's impossible for me to select leaders who, in some way, don't reflect me. Some of them have reached iconic status, others are pioneering significant change in their chosen field. Most of us have faced the likeability barriers that are key to this discussion. As I'll show in the following chapters, some were easy to write about, others presented challenges. All, I truly believe, are worth talking about for the purpose of giving a well-rounded view of the issues that feed into leader likeability. That said, they are examples: please consider them alongside other leaders you know of to draw your own conclusions.

TASK: Take some time to consider your role within the system.

What influence can you have on changing the system? How does the system shape perceptions of you, or others?

'Toot Sweet' Recap

1. Stepping into our unlikeability enables us to explore ourselves, holistically, from a place of empowerment, rather than a place of fear.

2. Our reactions to others are a reflection of ourselves and vice versa.

3. Our perceived unlikeability is linked to the privileges and disadvantages which flow from conforming to or challenging the status quo.

CHAPTER FOUR

The Brand Promise

What is a brand?

How many of us see a brand as one of those ambiguous things that all the experts tell us we need - something we've tried to build for our own business, but without really grasping what it's all about. Did you put your hand up?

Some people think branding is a modern day 'quack' idea, but the truth is, human beings are made to brand: we've been branding since the beginning of time. In 2015, Lippincott (a creative consultancy which has worked with some of the world's most memorable brands) staged an exhibition about the history of branding at the Design Museum in London. It highlighted how branding exists in nature (for example, natural markings on insects or animals,) and links the first human branding with cave drawings.

An article about the exhibition explains:

"Cave paintings show some of the first examples of how humans transcribed their world into visual representations that have deeper meaning. Despite lacking direct translation, the decorated walls are an important demonstration of how our Homo Sapien ancestors were hard-wired to brand."[21]

The exhibition covered other forms of branding, such as cattle branding from 2,700BC, the ichthys (fish) sign used by early Christians, as well as individual marks bakers pressed into bread in early Roman times. Personal branding has been traced back at least as far as Napoleon, who used his hat to create a unique image. Formal, protected, product brands date back to 1876 and morphed into corporate identities before evolving further into more human-centric ecosystems. Brands are both a personal expression of the people behind them, as well as a personal validation for those enjoying them. In the modern world, our brand is a binary expression of our identity and our customer's experience.

Let's consider the everyday items you use going about your daily activities and why you chose them. What kind of pens do you use? Are they the cheapest pens you can find, scattered all about the house? Do you use multi-colours? Are you addicted to highlighting?

Do you drink tea from any old mug you can find on the run, or do you sit down and enjoy the experience of drinking freshly brewed, exotic tea from a beautiful china cup?

What kind of music do you listen to, and what does it tell us about your story?

What kind of plants are in your garden? How well maintained is your lawn? What kind of art do you have on the walls? Do you have the cheapest furniture and knick-knacks that fill a space and serve a purpose? Or do you collect timeless treasures that can be handed down?

What shampoo is sitting in your shower? What car do you drive?

All of these seemingly minor and mundane details tell striking stories about who you are and what you value. Their brand is, essentially, part of your brand, in that you see part of yourself in those things. People often approach branding from a perspective of needing to 'create' a brand and this puts the brand outside of themselves. Often, they'll try to second-guess the market, and this can lead them astray. The answers actually begin within us. Our brand begins with us. It's part of our fabric as human beings.

Allow me to explain further.

Once upon a time, a corporation would simply put their brand on the table in front of the customer and walk away. Imagine someone coming up to you and saying, "We are the baker of the best cakes!" and ending the conversation there. Branding, today, is a two-way conversation. The brand talks to the market, the market talks back to, and about, the brand. It's not that these conversations didn't happen before, but they were much less visible and influential than they are today. This new way of thinking about brands helps us to determine the difference between a brand and a reputation.

Overall, a brand is a strategically built (internal or external) picture of you, based on many different factors relating to your business, leadership approach and personal brand. It says: "This is who I am, what I stand for, how I approach my work, and here are the benefits I offer to my clients that differ from my competitors."

A reputation is what you are known for, that is, what you've already delivered for your ideal clients, and how they articulate that value. For example, "I worked with Sally. She was great because... It helped me because... Before I worked with her things were like this.... Now they are like this.... I'd highly recommend her." Interestingly, the value we think we deliver for clients can often differ from their perceived benefits. Reputation contributes to brand. It's crucial. When we focus only on the brand, and have a one-way conversation, we lose sight of reputation - we're talking, but not listening. That damages our brand in the long term. We must deliver what we promise, not only in what we do, but who we are.

When we don't listen to the people who buy into our brand, and understand what they value about it, we can lose our moorings. For example, I was chatting to an associate of mine who has built quite a successful personal brand. Key attributes of her personal brand include her witty nature and direct way of speaking, complete with swearing. She constantly receives feedback that she has to stop swearing. In fact, people have told her they can't hire her for keynote speeches because she swears.

She said to me:

"I was hired for a keynote and got up on stage, and I didn't swear. At the end of the event, someone came up to me and said, 'Your talk was great, but I'm disappointed you didn't swear.'"

She had built a brand on the promise of being a particular kind of leader. By putting a lid on who she truly was to appease people she had never met, she unintentionally didn't deliver on that promise to someone who bought in to her brand. She learnt that her ideal clients want her to swear! They value it. It means something to them. That's part of what they love about her and what they buy from her.

Another misunderstanding that often occurs with branding is thinking that it's all about our physical assets. For example: what we wear, our photographs, logo, website, and branding colours. These are all important, but they only tell part of the story. Today, a successful brand must be an authentic expression of our identity, including: how we position ourselves as an authority, our leadership skills, how we strategize, how we demonstrate thought leadership, the experience we give our clients, our quality of thinking, our corporate behaviour and our distinctiveness in the market.

Think of the physical assets like the shell, and the rest as the soft, scrumptious crab meat underneath. We need the whole crustacean to be compelling. If you sell a spectacular-looking shell with nothing inside, you're not going to have happy customers. For example: you can have all the pretty branding shots in the world, but it's meaningless if, as a leader, you lack effective conflict management skills. If you're going to put Chilli Crab on the menu, you have to deliver on your promise. When diners crack that crab shell open, they have to find lots of delicious, meaty flesh. It's the same with your brand. All the bells and whistles of 'branding' might bring the customers to your table, but unless they find value and substance and the 'flavour' of something truly delicious and unique, they won't stay.

Where does customer connection fit in?

We've all heard that customer connection is vital in branding and can determine whether customers buy from you or not.

Brand designer Timothy Ingram says:

"Connection is as valuable as capital. Customer experience is as valuable as consistency. Consumers now control the brand narrative."[22]

Consider buying a house. You walk in and, if the house is presented in a way that tickles your fancy, you'll start to imagine yourself and your family in the house; using the house. You'll think: "We'll put our lamp there, our outdoor dining suite would look amazing there..." Yes, you love the house. But what you love more is "you" in the house; what being in the house means about you, what living in this neighbourhood offers you (and your family). This is true whether you're buying into a product or a person.

As with everything, there are exceptions. The decision to buy can be driven by other factors. Ron Malhotra, a wealth specialist, explained the concept of 'customer intrigue' in a vlog. Reiterating a conversation he had with someone named Ivan about the purchase of a Ferrari, he says:

"I said to Ivan, 'Ivan, if I'm selling you a $500,000 Ferrari for $25,000 and you hate me, are you not going to buy it?' Bullshit he won't buy it! If it's a deal, it's a deal, if there's value, there's value.'[23]

Now, I'm not sure about you, but if someone offered me a Ferrari for 25k, my first reaction would be, "What's wrong with the Ferrari?"

That aside, in this example, the person they are buying from is irrelevant. Yes, the buyer is attracted to the Ferrari brand, itself. But whether they like the individual selling the car or not, that is not going to deter them from the legitimate deal of a lifetime. Of course, the buyer might turn down the deal because of the product quality, or the trustworthiness of the seller (is the car stolen?!). It's possible that if the seller was truly vile and a similar deal, at a slightly higher price, was available elsewhere, the buyer might wear the extra cost for a better buying experience. But if it can be established it's a legitimate and legal sale at that astoundingly low price, who would turn down a deal like that to pay full price up the road because they don't like the salesperson? Would you?

Buying is ultimately a lottery of priorities for the customer. They will always be motivated to buy what is in their best interests. If they're buying a commodity, whatever is quicker, more convenient, better quality or value, a more enjoyable experience, etc, will always win, unless the only variable left is to compare the sellers themselves. But, when it comes to personal services, such as choosing a doctor or personal advisor, the 'commodity' is the seller, themselves. In these cases, the deciding factor, then, may well be the relationship between buyer and seller.

A trend in branding is for large corporations to bring in influencers or ambassadors to humanise their brands. Take, for example, Jamie Oliver working with Australian supermarket Woolworths. As with other celebrities, the idea is if you 'like' Jamie, you will naturally extend that affection to the brand he represents. But again, what happens if we despise Jamie Oliver and find ourselves desperate for milk and bread without any other supermarket nearby except Woolies? Would we refuse to shop there? Would we drive completely out of our way for miles to shop at a rival - even if it was more expensive - purely because of our dislike for Jamie? It would have to be some deep-seated hatred to spend all that extra time and money, or to miss out on coffee and Vegemite toast in the morning!

So, what does this mean for aiming to be likeable?

When we are true to ourselves and understand how to position our value, we don't need to 'aim' to be likeable. We will naturally connect with those who dig us. To the contrary, when we aim to be likeable, we dilute our brand. We miss the people who want to buy into us for who we truly are. Instead, we attract clients who will ultimately never be truly satisfied with who we are, how we work and what we deliver. A key symptom of this is that businesses end up with a revolving door of clients. The business might have a great brand, but if, at the core of the brand (remember the crab meat?) the human component isn't 'the real article', their reputation starts to unravel. Being distinctive is impossible if you're not prepared to be unlikeable.

By freeing ourselves from the shackles of trying to be liked by everyone, we stop doing things in a bid to elicit a certain response or outcome (i.e. acceptance). Instead, we start doing things we truly believe in, are passionate about and have a talent for. The results become an organic by-product of that, not an end in themselves. Thus, we begin to see ourselves and our role as leaders in a whole new light. Delivering on our brand promise becomes easy, because we're delivering on our true selves!

TASK: Define your brand promise. What do you want to be known for delivering?

CHAPTER FIVE

The False Equivalency

The problem with likeability in a 'mass appeal' leadership sense is its allure.

Likeability, as it relates to charisma, is often assumed to equate to effective leadership. After all, the charismatic leader can gather an almost cultish following - admirers who are seemingly hooked on every word and every move. Charismatic, or likeable leaders, can paint an incredible vision and quickly gain buy-in. Following them, and being in their presence, is so enjoyable it's intoxicating. Sometimes it's so electrifying we become blind to their ineffectiveness. You see, likeable leaders know exactly which buttons to push to enhance loyalty. They're incredibly compelling, but such power can be superficial.

That's not to say that charisma is bad, of course. Charisma is a quality that can enhance effective leadership when it's combined with other leadership skills and qualities. The ability to influence is powerful, which is a good thing when it's used for good. But what about when it's used for harm? Think: Hitler (leader of the Nazi regime), Jim Jones (the civil rights preacher, faith healer and socialist cult leader who inspired mass suicide), and Charles Manson (a cult leader whose members committed murder).

Where things go awry is when we read charisma, in isolation, as a leadership capability without critically assessing the leader as a whole. When we are seduced by a charismatic leader, we tend to overblow their achievements and underplay their faults: "But he's so great. I really like him." This can lead to a long hangover as we come to terms with how, in reality, the leader didn't live up to expectations.

A client of mine recalled being called in to help mop up the fallout from a charismatic leader who was hired with the expectation his huge social media presence would create opportunities for the company. But his number one priority was his own status. He occupied his time positioning his brand, internally and externally, instead of getting on with the business of leading. His preoccupation about how people viewed him meant he lacked the courage to paint a clear vision, he didn't spend time on governance, and he was unable to engage in the hard conversations needed to take the organisation to the next level. My client estimated that, by the time she arrived to remedy the situation, the organisation was about 6 months away from total collapse. She explained that this particular leader certainly had charisma but coupled with narcissistic traits. This proved hugely divisive as staff and clients took sides - either passionately with him or militantly against him. He was brilliant at branding with 'shiny words' but when the cracks started to show there was no substance beneath the shell, and he made a quick exit to avoid taking responsibility.

It's quite common for charismatic leaders to burn brightly for a short period of time before their light fades. This is because likeability and mass appeal will only get us so far. It serves a particular purpose for a short period of time and is good for achieving a single goal. Long-term leadership performance requires a different set of skills and qualities, some of them not overly sexy. Contrary to popular belief, influence does not always equal quality of thinking or character - although it goes without saying that not all charismatic leaders intend to do harm. We are so obsessed with the charismatic leader that we love the easy-to-package stars who are great on camera and present an archetypal brand story we can't help but buy into.

Example: rags to riches.

A charismatic iconic leader for us to consider is none other than Nelson Mandela. When Mandela died in 2013, he was remembered as a one-of-a-kind leader, perhaps one of the most likeable leaders in history. Mandela is usually cast as a legendary hero; an exemplar of someone who arose from adversity as a changed man and faced the world full of peace, forgiveness, wisdom and love. Mandela won global adulation as a man who wasn't angry about being jailed for 27 years as a freedom fighter but walked free with a steely determination to change the world peaceably. Mandela was responsible for ending apartheid; the forced segregation of black and white South Africans. He achieved the seemingly impossible in 5 years after being elected as President in 1994 - a feat that deserves the widespread acknowledgment and admiration it has received.

But was Mandela "the brand" truly representative of Mandela the leader?

The author of the book Likenomics, Rohit Bhargava, points out:

"People didn't follow Mandela because of the ideas; they followed him because of him. When he invited you over for tea and listened to your concerns, and then spoke, you couldn't help trusting his vision."[24]

Mandela's brand encapsulates the kind of person we all wish we could be. Like the holy, pure version of ourselves that we put on a pedestal. If he could achieve it, we could all strive to be better people. But as the saying goes, there are two sides to every story, and in the case of Mandela, that's very much true. In the course of his lifetime, Mandela was both a violent revolutionary and a diplomatic statesman.

As Danny Schechter wrote for Al Jazeera in 2011:

"[Mandela] was an easy-to-market brand... And quickly became the focus of media attention. Soon, there were songs, concerts, TV documentaries and marches. He became the best-known prisoner in the world."

Schechter refers to Mandela as *"... a saint cleaned up, sanitised and repackaged for mass consumption."*[25]

Mandela's biographer, John Carlin, has described Mandela's diplomatic meetings with the white Afrikaners who hated his guts as, *"the most unlikely exercise in political seduction ever undertaken."*[26]

In 2013, Mark Gevisser wrote in The New Daily:

"He made a fetish of his biography. As he was in chains, so too was South Africa; as he managed to negotiate himself into freedom, so too could his country; as he forgave his oppressors and his adversaries, so too should his compatriots."

Gevisser continues:

"In his long political career, he was immensely creative, but by no means saintly: he has been a trickster, an operator, a maverick. He might have had an extraordinary instinct, but he was unabashedly instrumentalist. He did not take a step—do a jig—without calculating the odds. And these odds were often set by realpolitik, rather than a moral compass. More important, Mandela's perceived sanctity has had a powerful effect, not always positive, on the growth of the democracy he played so great a role in nurturing."[27]

Mandela's daughter, Maki Mandela, says:

"I'm very proud that he dedicated his life to creating a better society. Not that he was perfect or a saint in any way."[28]

What many people don't know, or choose to ignore about Mandela, is that he was a radical fighter involved in violent clashes to overthrow the government. He wasn't only jailed for being a political prisoner, but also for being instrumental in planning fatal bombings.

Were his actions justified given the climate at the time? This is a hard question to answer. In one way, it's hard to justify violence. In another, there are circumstances where a seemingly non-violent person could be justifiably driven to violence. For example, if someone was trying to murder you, you'd defend yourself at all costs, right? Or what if someone was trying to harm your children? Granted, there's a difference between self-defence and pre-meditating a crime that results in the death of others, but the context matters. In the case of Mandela, the violent uprising was in response to the South African government's use of violence on black protesters. Prior to that it had been a peaceful affair.

As Olivia B Waxman wrote for TIME in 2018:

"That's when the Sharpeville Massacre took place. In 1960, South African police killed 69 black protesters in the town 40 miles south of Johannesburg; amid

the crackdown that followed, the government banned the ANC. As the ANC went underground, Mandela became the head of the military wing of the African National Congress, Umkhonto we Sizwe (Spear of the Nation), also known as MK. In 1964, he was convicted of sabotage and treason, and wound up imprisoned until 1990. TIME later described the group's activities from 1962 as 'low-level guerrilla war.'"[29]

Mandela was subsequently placed on terror watch lists. When, post-prison, 'brand Mandela' was launched, 'militant Mandela' was conveniently smudged out. Was he being disingenuous? No. The charismatic part of his personality seemed to be genuine, and Mandela himself never denied the truth of who he was.

Writing for the LA Times in 2013, Robyn Dixon revealed an excerpt from a letter Mandela wrote to his second wife, Winnie:

"We are told that a saint is a sinner who keeps on trying to be clean. One may be a villain for three-quarters of his life and be canonized because he lived a holy life for the remaining quarter of that life.'[30]

Mandela wasn't a saint, but he wasn't exactly a sinner either. Could prison have changed him? Undoubtedly. Could he have been playing the role he thought he had to, in order to achieve the desired outcome? Yes, that's possible - and it was certainly effective for that particular change. How great were Mandela's leadership skills? Given his short tenure, we can't be sure how well he would have fared over a longer period of time in political office. He has received criticism for some of the political deals he brokered as well as how he shaped a transformation which left holes that South Africa will long be trying to fill.

As Fred Bridgland points out in The Scotsman:

"When he became president, he rubbed shoulders with and took big donations from some dubious statesmen, including Libya's Muammar Gaddafi, Cuba's Fidel Castro and Indonesia's president Suharto."[31]

South African academic, Alan Hirsch (professor and director of the Graduate School of Development Policy, University of Cape Town) says:

"The ANC's promised economic transformation has been disappointing in several ways. Poverty hasn't reduced quickly enough, inequality remains at world-beating levels, and the pace of growth has, on average, been pedestrian. It is currently

glacial. It is quite likely that decisions made during the transition, before and after 1994, contributed to this outcome.'[82]

It's fair to say Mandela certainly wasn't the 'perfect' leader he was purported to be. His skills were advantageous as a leader of a movement, but that is entirely different to serving as a political leader dealing with everything from mundane government tasks to international diplomacy. Of course, we can't ask him now, but Mandela may well have known his limitations and did his best to do his part before passing the baton.

It begs the question, how many skilled but seemingly 'unlikeable' leaders have we overlooked in the corporate environment, at the voting booth, or for other opportunities, simply because we 'like' someone else more? And how does aiming to be likeable impact our leadership performance?

Well. Let's ask ourselves this: how many times have we made decisions based on what increases our standing in society, over truly serving the markets we lead? How many actions or inactions have we been responsible for, based solely on wanting to be liked? How many conversations have we avoided, or what feedback have we withheld, because we didn't want to make ourselves unpopular? Holding back 'uncomfortable truths' is ultimately a disservice to clients, staff, and colleagues. It's false economics. If you think back to those who had a meaningful impact on your life, was it the person who was enjoyable to be around, or the one who challenged you to be better?

When we aim to be popular, or likeable, we might solve short-term problems while amplifying long-term ones. In fact, in our roles as leaders there are times when we are required to make unpopular decisions for the overall survival of a business or society. Being effective leaders requires us to navigate this well and put aside our desire to be liked, in order to serve. Yes! It requires us to be unlikeable!

What many leaders fail to understand, and what I see frequently with clients, is a deep concern that having difficult conversations or making unpopular decisions will damage relationships with their staff or their clients. When we try to preserve relationships instead of prioritising effective leadership, our interactions with clients or staff may be enjoyable, but not as meaningful or productive. The truth of the matter is that if conflict is managed well, it can enhance and strengthen relationships. Trying to avoid the hard conversation or outcome is often doing a disservice to clients. It allows important feedback to go unsaid, expectations to be misaligned, and tensions to escalate. Often the original problem ends up bigger than Ben Hur.

Through trying to avoid the conflict, we make the conflict worse! In addition, we risk our client or staff relationships drifting into the friend zone, which impacts our ability to help them achieve individual and collective goals. They become displeased with our leadership, don't respect boundaries, time, authority and in some cases, in the absence of effective leadership, can essentially take matters into their own hands to establish a de-facto self-governing body. This doesn't mean we have to run a dictatorship in order to be successful. Leadership styles have evolved from the hierarchical approach of the past. But there's a difference between being collaborative in leadership and striking the right balance between nurture and challenge, and favouring short term pleasantries over long-standing substantial outcomes.

It all comes down to how we view conflict, and how we utilise it to help people to be their best. When we break it down, conflict is simply telling us there is a problem to be solved. Discomfort is often the catalyst for growth, and friction is the impetus for cohesion. Part of productive leadership is being able to facilitate such a change journey, not merely hand out band-aids and ice packs along the course of one race.

True leadership power, within the context of this book, goes beyond the pretty trimmings of cosmetic influence that's trotted out time and time again - especially with the rise of social media. It asks us to look deeper within ourselves. What do we really want? How do we want to be remembered? It's one thing to have a legacy, but it's another to have a legacy and imprint on the world that withstands the test of time. The latter involves embracing our unlikeability in ways that are kinder and more empowering than we could ever have imagined.

TASK: Get clear on what aiming for likeability gives you, as well as how much it's currently costing you.

CHAPTER SIX

◇◇◇

The Gender Penalty

Regardless of an individual's gender or sexual identify, gender bias punishes anyone who bucks traditional gender norms by branding them 'unlikeable'.

It can be hard to accept that a person, or group of people, could find you unlikeable based on something as inherent as how you inhabit your gender. And as I will show in this book, gender is not the only personal attribute that contributes to unfair perceptions of unlikeability.

Research supports the contention that when a person steps outside stereotypical gender norms, they are more likely to be considered unlikeable.[33]

Take women for example. The more successful they appear to be, the less they are liked. The more they display traits that are typically perceived as masculine (e.g. being confident, assertive, motivated by money, successful in business, or exhibiting power-seeking behaviours) the more they are seen as 'unlikeable.'[34]

The same can be said for men who display feminine traits; for example, being vulnerable, sensitive, communal, supportive or otherwise 'effeminate' vs. demonstrating macho masculinity.[35] Even the simple act of a man asking for help can cause him to be viewed as a less competent leader.[36]

On the topic of competency, study after study demonstrates that competent women are consistently rated as lacking social skills, when compared to similarly competent men.[37] Studies have shown that, in a leadership capacity, women are seen as having a 'take care' function, while men are seen to have a 'take charge' role.[38]

Contrary to popular belief, women CEOs are not terminated from poorly performing companies at higher rates than men.[39] They are, however, more likely to be appointed to an organisation that's already performing poorly.[40] They're also 45 per cent more likely to be terminated from a company that's performing well, even if they were originally appointed to turn it around and succeeded.[41]

The difference between male and female terminations from poorly performing organisations is statistically insignificant. But researchers have observed that news stories are far more likely to linger expansively on the reasons why a departing female CEO has 'failed' while marking the termination of a male CEO with far less fanfare. This means we hear far more about female CEOs being fired than their masculine peers. What's even more interesting is that, even though female reporters are more likely to write about women, it doesn't reduce the bias in reporting.[42]

While women are credited for displaying empathy in leadership, men are not. Yet while men aren't penalised for not displaying empathy in leadership, women are.[43] Frankly, it all comes down to outdated notions about gender and gender roles in leadership. That is, meanings that are actually meaningless.

What do I mean by that?

Well, let's take masculinity as an example. What we think of today as 'masculine' has certainly changed over time. For example, a man wearing a pink business shirt today wouldn't raise an eyebrow, but it would have before the 1970s when 'real men' wore only white shirts and staid ties.

Concepts of 'masculinity' and 'femininity' vary across cultures, time, and according to a person's age. There may be competing ideas about what signifies masculinity, even within societies themselves. In other words, masculinity is a social construct (as is femininity).

When we look at the history of gender identity, high heels were originally only worn by men - they were a status symbol of masculinity! High heels, first worn by horsemen, were later worn at court, rather than on a horse, because status was associated with clothing that lacked practical purpose. INTERESTINGLY (and I've hit the caps button because this revelation blew my mind), women began wearing high heels to look more masculine. According to Elizabeth Semmelhack of the Bata Shoe Museum in Toronto:

"In the 1630s you had women cutting their hair, adding epaulettes to their outfits. They would smoke pipes, they would wear hats that were very masculine. And this is why women adopted the heel - it was in an effort to masculinise their outfits."[44]

Similarly, while make-up is now considered 'feminine' and men who use it, generally, as unmanly or at least, androgynous, this was not always the case.

According to Amanda Montell in Byrdie:

"For millennia, stretching from 4000 BCE through the 18th century, men traditionally used makeup in myriad ways. It wasn't until the mid-1800s that makeup was relegated to one end of the gender spectrum... Roman men were known to apply red pigment to their cheeks, lighten their skin with powder, and paint their nails using a stomach-turning elixir of pig fat and blood... [In Elizabethan England] makeup was wildly popular among men, who valued ghost-white powdered skin."[45]

Today, the men in Chad's Wodaabe tribe attract brides with their elaborate make-up and wide smiles to show off their beautiful teeth.[46]

The idea that little boys should dress differently from little girls in order to distinguish their gender is a relatively modern idea. Young children's clothing was identical until well into the nineteenth century, mainly for practical reasons like economics and potty training. While pink is now seen as a signifier for femininity (blue is for boys, pink is for girls), not long ago it was the opposite. In 1918, The Ladies' Home Journal advised their readers that:

"The generally accepted rule is pink for the boys, and blue for the girls. The reason is that pink, being a more decided and stronger color, is more suitable for the boy, while blue, which is more delicate and dainty, is prettier for the girl."[47]

Many believe that our gender differences are based in our sex differences, or biology. While there are some biological differences between the sexes, they are not as significant as many would have us believe. There is more diversity across sexes than between them and just because a gene exists, doesn't mean it's switched on. How we evolve, biologically, is influenced by our environment and culture; and as demonstrated in the examples here, we are adaptable.[48] What's considered masculine in Australia is different to the Wodaabe tribe in Africa. What's considered masculine in 2019 is different to 1918.

The meanings a society uses to define masculinity and femininity as a form of social control are in fact meaningless in reality. They are made up, a 'trend' of the time, sentiment, and place. This doesn't mean gender labels in themselves are meaningless, quite the opposite. But biological sex should not be confused with an individual's expression of their gender. People should not be required to comply with arbitrary expectations about how they should behave because of their biological sex.

A powerful example of this is the way that hairdresser, podcaster, and television celebrity, Jonathan Van Ness, corrected a media outlet which printed an article with the title: *"Men in gender non-binary outfits are trending at MTV VMA's 2019."*

Van Ness tweeted the article, saying: *"For me, it's actually a non binary person in a non binary outfit."*[49]

The title of the article has since been updated to: *"Celebrating Gender Non-Conformist Style in Bold Looks at the VMAs."*[50]

Policing gender conformity isn't restricted to men. Studies show women also enforce gender stereotypes (on both sexes), sometimes more harshly than men.[51] Reading this made me emotional. I saw so much of myself in this. While I do have many traits that are considered 'feminine' by today's standards, many of my traits are also 'masculine' and not 'becoming' of a woman. It made me realise that my unlikeability issue was deeply personal; far more personal than I could ever have imagined.

When considering how the gender penalty impacts male leaders, it's hard to go past the curious case of politician, Bill Shorten. At the time of writing, he wouldn't be considered an iconic leader per se, and his political journey is still unfolding. However, he presents an interesting example to contemplate.

In 2017, Anne Summers wrote for The Sydney Morning Herald:

"You hear it all the time, people saying, 'There's something about Bill Shorten I just don't like.' The party's polling shows it, as does the government's. People can't necessarily put their finger on precisely what it is. Some will say it's his voice, or his delivery, his lame zingers, or the way he shouts when he's giving a speech. Others say that he's not trustworthy, or that he is unauthentic."[52]

Various comments in online discourse have also labelled Shorten as "weak." Despite various allegations of criminal activity, he has never been charged or found guilty. Yet, there are still concerns about his trustworthiness.

We know it can't be "his lame zingers" or "the way he shouts when he's giving a speech" because Prime Minister Scott Morrison, who defeated Bill Shorten in the 2019 Federal election, has received similar criticisms. And sure, the allegations of criminal activity can understandably taint a brand, but he isn't the only politician whose actions and integrity have been brought into question.

In fact, when we pull apart all the reasons given for why Shorten, supposedly, isn't likeable, there's nothing overly compelling to hang our hat on. Except when we sift through the feedback, we can't help but notice it's peppered with criticisms related to traits that could be categorised as feminine; traits that former Prime Ministers either lacked, or suppressed, to the benefit of their reputations as 'strong leaders'. Is this the crux of the problem for Shorten: Hard-nosed and masculine denotes strength while soft-hearted and feminine signifies weakness?

A key criticism of Shorten is his supposed need for love and acceptance - that his 'neediness' erodes confidence in his competence and authority. Quoted in David Marr's 2015 profile of Shorten in the Quarterly Essay, Margaret Simons says:

"'Bill Shorten likes to be liked, and he is good at it too... His weakness, say those who know him, is that he needs to bask in the glow of others' love and admiration. He needs to be loved.'"

Marr continues:

"In the rough and tumble of the party, his pursuit of affection can seem a little desperate. 'It really drives him nuts when someone doesn't like him,' a leading adversary in the faction wars told me. 'He has to be loved. Even when he fucks you over, he wants you to like him – he rings and tries to make up.'"

Marr goes on to contrast Shorten with former Prime Minister Hawke, who sadly passed away just before the 2019 election:

"Shorten doesn't thrive on hostility. It's hard to imagine him staring down the unions as Hawke did to open the Australian economy to the world. It's hard to see him trying to persuade Australia to change its mind on any great issue. He is not another Bob Hawke, sitting above the fray, relying on his lieutenants to bring him the numbers."

To conclude this discussion, Marr insists:

"It isn't true he stands for nothing. There's a list of decent Labor policies he's always backed: jobs, prosperity, education and health. What's counted against him is he stands for nothing brave.'[53]

The bravery comment sticks out like a sore thumb. Would we require a female politician to present 'brave' policies in order to be considered worthy? Or would being 'brave' work against her? Would we also judge a woman who was concerned about being liked? Or would we expect that of her? If Shorten were a woman and didn't chase likeability, what judgments would we draw about him (her) then?

The comment about how Shorten avoids hostile interactions is also interesting. According to business academics David Knight and Maria Tullberg, in macho-masculine contexts the expression of hostility:

"... becomes a powerful means to keep discipline to sustain male bonding in ways that help secure a stable masculine identity."[54]

We can easily see how men who buck this norm could be considered unmanly, and therefore, "weak" or "soft." Research shows it can be enough for a man to simply support feminism to rock that masculine identity to the core.[55] Could it be true that people saw Shorten's tendency to be more agreeable and collegiate as a weakness? Was he penalised because these are characteristics we expect of female leaders? Did Shorten's support of women and feminism go against him? Has his hang-up about being likeable undermined his credibility rating? Surely, regardless of gender, the ability to compromise, collaborate and be amicable is just as much a leadership strength as being willing to 'storm the barricades'?

How do we overcome a barrier like this?

If we head back to Ichiro Kishimi and Fumitake Kogo and The Courage to Be Disliked, there is a very relevant and insightful passage which focuses on the question: "Whose task is this?"

The Philosopher said to his student:

"In general, all interpersonal relationship troubles are caused by intruding on other people's tasks, or having one's own tasks intruded on. Carrying out the separation of tasks is enough to change one's interpersonal relationships dramatically."[56]

In plain language, when we stop making other people's tasks (or stuff) about us, then it stops being about us. It might be directed at us, but is it about us, or them? Sometimes it might be about us, in which case, we have personal responsibility to deal with that. But at other times it's theirs and not ours to worry about. These words stuck in my mind because it's a concept I often discuss with clients. Instead of asking them whose task it is, we explore where their responsibility begins and ends. Sometimes my clients will take on problems that aren't theirs, and other times they will deny responsibility for issues they've created.

Without realising it, I had been absorbing other people's gender bias and prejudice as mine to deal with; like a vessel taking on water. This was a big 'what the fuck' moment of truth. I used to think that people-pleasers were only those super-agreeable people who never coloured outside the lines - people who would simply agree with others in conversations, toe the line, and take the path of least resistance. And yet I'd consider myself less agreeable on the spectrum (although not totally disagreeable), and here I was, lassoed by people-pleasing. It never occurred to me that even 'unlikeable' people like me might also be 'people-pleasers'. I realised it shows up in different ways for different people. For me, while I wasn't overtly a people-pleaser and wouldn't placate people in interactions, I'd secretly agonise about how unpleasing I was, while devising elaborate strategies to turn my unpleasantness into a pleasing quality.

Here's the clincher to this epiphany:

People-pleasers used to grind me, especially where I felt they were being obsequious or inauthentic. And yet, I WAS ONE. I was grinding myself, and I didn't even know it. Ha!

I decided to stop taking on water immediately. I also decided to stop justifying myself or trying to convince people of my worth. In doing so, I stopped asking for people's permission to exist and I simply started existing. I made a rule that I wasn't going to outsource my worthiness to the standards of others, unless their standards mattered: for example, the standards of my best clients - the ones who have put money on the table and invested in our relationship together. I put a framework in place where I defined what feedback mattered, what required a response and what didn't. Thinking back to the woman at that networking event, and her comments about 'not buying from those she doesn't like': if I could live that moment over, I'd take the opportunity to talk about what the research tells us about unlikeability - not because I'd feel a need to justify myself, but because now I wouldn't simply assume her comments were about me.

In all of my interactions I began to recognise how much people reveal about themselves in their feedback. I started seeing other people, instead of just myself all the time. I also started wondering what I might be here to teach those who dislike me. Previously, I would have asked myself what I could learn from another person or experience. But what if it was me who was destined to teach them something, just by being who I am? Of course, whether they are open to that lesson is entirely up to them. And whether they take the lesson on is none of my business. Regardless, the learning opportunity is there.

I'm not the only leader encouraging others to express their unique identity, and I'm certainly not the most notable. I don't want to paint myself as some kind of messiah in this space. But I understand the significance of the contribution of being a role model in my own unique way; whether that be in person-to-person interactions or to a mass audience.

These personal insights led me to the pivotal moment when I started to think about iconic leaders; the kind of change-makers who carve out the trenches for the rest of us, those who are changing or have changed the world for the better, the most loved and the most famous. What made them distinctive? What obstacles did they face? How did unlikeability play into the success of their brand? What can they teach us?

The answers surprised me. They may just surprise you too.

TASK: Ask yourself: If none of the gender rules existed, who would you be? What mix of masculine and feminine qualities feel most aligned with you?

_____

_____

_____

_____

_____

_____

'Toot Sweet' Recap:

1. Being true to ourselves is delivering on our brand promise.
2. Charisma, alone, is not evidence of true leadership power.
3. Labels are important, but their true meaning lies in how we identify ourselves and express our truth.

CHAPTER SEVEN

Grappling with a Unique Mind

I've always had a unique ability to pull things apart and see them in interesting ways. This has been both a benefit and a detriment to my professional life.

In my corporate days I found it nearly impossible to do my job without wanting to change the world in the process. I have always been a problem solver, not a task-ticker. If there is a more efficient, effective, strategic way to do something, I'll be 'on it like Sonic'. This means that I'd always be on a mission with various projects to add what I saw as 'real value.' In some environments this was appreciated. Like the time an email went around, "Can everyone use Shevonne's design for the training facilitation, please? It's great."

In other environments it was a source of bewilderment and frustration for everyone involved.

My mind: 'Why would you not want to do things better, more strategically, commercially, and save money here and here?'

My manager's mind: 'Why can't Shevonne just do her job?'

It was incredibly deflating at the time, but it's rather funny now that I look back on it.

I did not realise I was entrepreneurial, although the tell-tale signs were there. As a young child I was always setting up businesses; whether a doctor's office, hospital, school, clothing shop, or supermarket - there was always something going on. But in country Victoria in the 80s, entrepreneurism wasn't a concept I'd ever heard of. Careers advice very much centred around specific jobs; nurse, teacher, vet, etc. I remember in high school finding the process of trying to select one occupation to aim towards literally impossible.

"But I want to be a vet, forensic psychologist, lawyer, actor, astronaut, marry Prince William, plus be the next Celine Dion. Is there a career that meets that criteria?"

SIDE NOTE: Yes, I was a huge Celine Dion fan. Roxette was my first favourite band, followed by Salt-N-Pepa, but Celine is timeless. If you weren't a Celine fan, did you even 80s and 90s?

While I wasn't blessed with Celine's vocal cords, as an adult I realised I didn't have to choose. In fact, my propensity for gaining a variety of experiences in varying roles, businesses and cultures served me extremely well for the work I do in my entrepreneurial pursuits. Sure, I've acquired a diverse array of formal qualifications, and my husband has threatened me with divorce if I go back to university again (Pssttt! There's another area of interest I'm eyeing off - you know *nothing!*) but rather than lacking commitment, I am dedicated to experiencing and learning as much as I possibly can. I'm all for biting life off and chewing furiously while sauce runs down your chin.

This is all well and good now, but being a problem solver in a task-ticking environment is like putting Celine Dion in a heavy metal band. There's nothing against one approach compared to the other - it's more about finding an environment in which you can thrive.

When I started my own consulting business, my idiosyncratic mind became my biggest asset. It's what people buy from me - a mind with a unique ability to help them reinvent industries, flip everything on its head, and strategically position their distinctive brand. It's a mind that helps me to take my own businesses to new heights, including our global, luxury children's fashion brand, Stella Phoenix.

It sounds weird that people buy a mind - like some kind of brain in a bottle - but when we think about it, regardless of who we are, or what we're leading or creating, people are buying our minds. Lately, there's a shift from fetishizing "information", towards recognising the economic value of imagination and creativity; what we do with that information. According to Forbes:

"Where Science is the system of acquiring knowledge, art is the application of knowledge. Art can be defined as requiring a skill to conduct any human activity and as we are well aware, running a business involves a multitude of skills."[57]

Sales can mean the literal transaction of value or services for cash, but it can also mean the buy-in to a project, strategy, culture or movement. Sometimes it's one mind, other times it's the collective genius of many.

A successful leader I admire once said to me, "I purposefully surround myself with a team who will actively disagree with me. The ideas we end up implementing far surpass anything I'd ever come up with myself."

It's that kind of learning expert approach that really rocks my socks.

Let's consider the book you are reading right now. Sure, by buying this book you bought my mind, but you're also tapping into the minds of the experts and people we've quoted, my researcher who combed through the literature on this topic, my legal team who reviewed it, my graphics genius who took my ambiguous book design vision of, "I want something modern, but classic, but booky" and turned it into this beautiful text, my editor who proofread it, my publisher, the bookseller who was clever enough to stock this book, and of course, you. There are SO MANY unique minds involved in your learning process as you read through this book. Harnessing your unique mind for success means grappling with it - the good, the bad, the ugly - but also welcoming ideas that challenge your ego, your prejudices and your preconceptions.

How is any of this relevant to being unlikeable? Well, to be pioneers we must be prepared to be disliked. While, to some, our unique mind might create magic, others might see it as totally wacko. Because of this, we have a tendency to smother our unique mind with a pillow out of fear of judgement. Have you ever done that? Are you doing it right now? Your unique mind is part of your competitive value as a leader. Often unrealised, it provides fuel for your ultimate success. In order to utilise it, you must first understand the unique value your mind brings and find the right set of conditions, or ecosystem, that will help it thrive - kind of like a hothouse but less sweaty (unless you're a horticulturalist inventing new plant varieties or solving the world's food shortage). Your endeavour, your role, your business is simply how you put what's bubbling away inside your unique mind out into the world; like an artist trying to put what he sees with his mind's eye onto canvas, or a composer trying to transpose the music in her head into a musical score.

To illustrate, let's look at the poignant yet courageously inspirational story of Amy Winehouse.

Amy's leadership story is one I continually come back to. It's hard to write about such an iconic leader without fearing you won't do justice to her legacy and memory. (This is a hurdle I faced with pretty much every leader I've written about!) Recognised early as a strikingly talented writer, musician, and performer, Amy Winehouse's journey began with promise. She refused to conform to the music industry. Instead, she created music to reflect her own unique style and perspective.

In 2011, Shirley Halperin from the Hollywood Reporter wrote about seeing Winehouse perform live:

"It was an uh-oh moment but also a thrilling one. Here was a talent unlike any we had seen in the post 9/11 era of politically correct, pristinely produced pop (your Ashlee Simpsons, Pussycat Dolls, etc) – one with grit and gravitas, who wasn't shy about using the 'C' word on stage, who sang from the depths of her soul, not to a metronome clicking in her head."[58]

Mark Cooper, head of BBC Music Television says:

"... There was only ever one Amy Winehouse. She was frank and fresh and haunted. And we miss her."[59]

And in a 2015 Interview with The Guardian, her manager, Nick Shymanksy, observed:

"In a world where artists can be quite safe and average at times, she was special."[60]

Amy was unlike other artists in her genre; that's a tell-tale sign of someone harnessing their unique mind. As another example, the other day someone described me as the 'anti-guru' in a world of motivational gurus, and I love it! What they meant was, rather than selling a short-term buzz with unsustainable strategies and tactics, I'm helping people to achieve realistic change by encouraging them to be themselves and work with what they've got.

Sadly, for Amy, the mind that made her unforgettable as an artist was the same mind that led to her ultimate demise. Amy battled addiction to the end, while also enduring the unprecedented intrusion of the media and the outside world as they fed insatiably on her fragility. The beauty she brought to the world is often sacrificed this way; the world has a propensity for cheering our best, brightest and most original stars to the top of the mountain, then throwing them into the volcano.

Elite Daily contributor Elena Cleaves wrote about Amy's unlikeability in 2015:

"When R&B/soul starlet Amy Winehouse began rocketing to fame, she was berated as a dirty and promiscuous 'crackhead', junkie' and 'drunk'. They were, no doubt, harmful terms that followed her past her demise. When addicts die, shocking numbers of people claim their lives should not be grieved, believing an addict's death (whether by overdose or not) is an inevitability he or she brought upon him or herself. The addicts are made to be the butt of jokes, their lives undervalued and seen as nothing but a goldmine of comedic material. An addict's life is belittled to nothing more than a mix of booze and syringes and cast away without honoring the good he or she did. Amy Winehouse has been made a joke for years, made into memes making cheap shots at her dismissal of rehab with, 'No, no, no.' Winehouse joined the unfortunate 27 Club, but she left behind a legacy of raw talent, soul and passion. Her perfectionist ways ensured she truly believed in what she was putting out to the public. She always made sure her music was true to herself."[61]

Ironically, and as Cleaves touched on, the tragedy of Amy's story was the inspiration for the pivotal album in her career, Back to Black. Notably, in the spirit of being 'true to herself', she famously sang of her decision not to go to rehab; a decision for which she may have paid the ultimate price. In a way, we all did. Amy produced such extraordinary music with a microphone in one hand and a demon-battling sword in the other. In fact, she often turned her pain into art.

Had the world truly appreciated Amy Winehouse's different shades and jaded beauty at the time, how different might the outcome have been? We'll never know - and in some ways, we can't get too lost in the 'what if' game. But while we would never wish addiction on anyone, those who dismiss Amy as a talent wasted are actually missing what she gave to the world. We can't deny Amy wouldn't have been the talent she was if she didn't channel her unique experiences into her music in the way she did. While it's easy to feel like Amy's potential was unfulfilled - and undoubtedly her loss has reverberated profoundly - her unique mind gave us more than we could have ever imagined. She was incredibly fractured and vulnerable, yet an awe-inspiring force of a woman.

In a 2004 interview with journalist John Marrs, Amy said:

"I'd like to be remembered as someone who wasn't satisfied with just one level of musicianship… As someone who was a pioneer."[62]

Whether you loved or loathed her music, Amy left a powerful and timeless legacy that expanded the boundaries of her craft. I will always remember her brilliance and distinctiveness and enjoy getting lost in her music. (Next time you hear an Amy Winehouse song, or plug in her album for a re-run, stop to savour her soul for a little longer.) The lessons that Amy's life-and-death struggle have to teach us will continue to come to light into the future. We'll also remember something much deeper about Amy. She was, after all, a window into our raw humanity - a humanity we all share, even the most famous of celebrities.

How does this relate to our personal leadership story?

We may not be addicts or musicians, but we all have a little piece of Amy within us to varying degrees. That is, we all face our own mortal struggles. We're all the artists of our own lives. Harnessing our unique mind requires us to embrace the paradoxical truth of who we are.

The common elements of the human psyche that people broadly understand and relate to are 'wisdom' and 'ego'. Some people say that stepping into our individual power means completely doing away with ego and operating entirely through the lens of wisdom. This 'all or nothing' approach can be counterproductive. It can lead people to fight against themselves rather than work with themselves.

We love to demonise ego even though it plays an important role in our survival and evolution (when it's given a specific project scope). Left to run unchecked though? All hell can break loose. Ego is like the well-meaning but pedantic friend who will risk-analyse the sweet cheeses out of our decisions. Staunchly loyal, rather than wanting to prevent us from achieving, our ego actually cares about us. It wants to keep us safe. We regularly blame undesirable traits like narcissism and gluttony on ego. But the ways in which our ego manifests depend on our personality and the circumstances. I've found that workshopping with ego is effective.

My Ego is the kind of character who really loves to have a say; she wants to be heard. Once she's said her piece, I find it easier to bring her off-sider, Wisdom, in to make a plan that satisfies all of us. The more I try to stifle my Ego, the more likely she is to escalate - like a toddler who asked for her sandwiches to be cut in triangles and changed her mind to squares when presented with the plate. Wisdom, for me, is free flowing - the inventor within, full of creativity, purpose, intuition and love. I seem to have a nerd with anxiety issues and a hippy cohabiting in my brain!

When I think of Wisdom and Ego, I imagine this old, odd, mismatched, but inseparable married couple sitting side by side in their colour coordinated moccasins. If we could interview them about the secrets of their everlasting romance, they would probably say they'd be lost without each other. Their 'relationship' works because they're opposites; the yin and yang. Without Wisdom, Ego would be rocking back and forth in the corner, a bottle of red wine in hand, burning holes in the curtains with cigarettes. Without Ego, Wisdom would be in a constant state of flux chasing one unbridled idea after another. But together? They work symbiotically. Wisdom paints the vision and Ego crunches the numbers. It's rather a cute love story.

While neuroscientists are hoping to find answers to formerly esoteric questions such as, "Where is the ego located in the brain?" and "Where does the brain store wisdom?" there is, as yet, no scientific consensus. The answers may depend on how we define these concepts. 'Ego' and

'Wisdom' almost certainly refer to a network of complex functions which may well occupy different parts of the brain. So, while there are some promising theories, these mysteries are not yet solved.

Getting back to my career crisis: I could have seen my indecisiveness as a fault (and frankly, I did at the time because I was unaware of the possibilities), or I could have stopped to ask myself, "What is this indecisiveness telling me, beyond the immediate decision? What strength, skill or lesson is it providing that can point me to my groove?" In other words, rather than seeing your mind as a burden, how can you realise its genius? How can you accept and take all the parts that make you, "you", and turn that into something meaningful to change the world for the better? This doesn't mean shirking responsibility for your mistakes, or putting aside your regrets, but rather asking yourself what beauty they've given you, and how you can apply that right now, in this moment, to create the movement you are destined to lead.

TASK: Like Amy turned her pain into art, what does your unique mind provide you with, right now, that you can turn into something meaningful to change the world?

_____

_____

_____

_____

_____

_____

_____

CHAPTER EIGHT

◇◇◇

Re-Birth

All the conversations about finding ourselves go along the lines of: We are born, we grow, we find ourselves, we die.

This one-dimensional description misses an important part of our life journey: evolution. It's not always a linear route. Sometimes we find ourselves multiple times in a lifetime, and other times, we find multiple parts of ourselves. There's not always a singular definition of who we are.

Lady Gaga is the perfect example of this.

Born Stefani Joanne Angelina Germanotta, at school, Lady Gaga was a laughing stock who was mocked for "being either too provocative or too eccentric."[63] She began her career gigging on the Lower East Side of New York and, as with other iconic brands we've seen, took the very thing she was judged for (provocation and eccentricity) and channelled it into her wildly successful album The Fame in 2008. Lady Gaga has never been widely understood, except by the fans who live and die by her quest to live her truth, and those who take the time to immerse themselves in her life as an artist. Lady Gaga is a walking, talking, breathing, transforming piece of living art; from what she wears, to what she sings, to how she describes her music, vision and life.

In a 2011 interview with Musicians at Google, Lady Gaga was asked whether she had heard from any of the people who used to bully her since she became famous. She recalled:

"One of the most awkward things that anyone ever said to me was, 'Well, my, my, how the tables have turned.'"[64]

Lady Gaga had gone from reviled to revered. In a 2019 Instagram post she says:

"I invented Lady Gaga. I found the superhero within me by looking in the mirror and seeing who I wanted to be."[65]

The idea of 'inventing' ourselves isn't to be confused with fabricating ourselves, and this is where much of the criticism sits with Gaga. Gaga expresses authentic parts of herself in her costumes or performance art that are so unusual, odd or freakish to others they find it hard to accept them as real. The meat dress (yes, it was made of real meat and later preserved as jerky) she wore at the 2010 MTV Video Music Awards is an example of this.

In The Courier-Mail in 2010, Jane Fynes-Clinton attacked Gaga, even while acknowledging her phenomenal success. She described Gaga as just:

"... some diva with a narcissistic disorder, a vacuous singer with a fat head and wallet who will do anything to grab page space and airplay."

Nevertheless, she concedes that:

"Lady Gaga is also the phenomenon of our time: the highest-selling singer, the most awarded pop princess, the queen of the video clip. She has an influence over the current wave of youth, whether we want her to or not. On Monday alone, she picked up eight [MTV Music] awards, dominating the ceremony."[66]

Despite her iconic success, Lady Gaga remains polarising, not only for her fashion or over-the-top performances, but also for her social advocacy. For example, she's been accused of advocating for minority groups she doesn't belong to. In a 2010 Sunday Times article, US cultural critic Camille Paglia accused Gaga of being:

"... more an identity thief than an erotic taboo breaker, a mainstream manufactured product who claims to be singing for the freaks, the rebellious and the dispossessed when she is none of those".[67]

Lady Gaga has maintained that her public persona is the authentic Stefani Germanotta; perhaps not the version of her that gets out of bed in the morning but nevertheless, 'stage Gaga' is an important and authentic part of who she has always been. Lady Gaga stands out from the crowd because she's developed the courage to embrace her oddball nature and show it. She explains:

"They said I was just weird, but really, I was just Born This Way."[68]

Why are we both drawn to and repelled by oddballs like Gaga?

When people hear the word 'oddball', they usually associate it with being a freak. By its very definition an oddball is 'strange or bizarre' compared to what's contextually 'normal.' A freak is linked to abnormality. While we relish the idea that we are 'one of a kind', we simultaneously struggle with that which is different and unexpected. Lady Gaga has become a mega-star by simultaneously shocking and inspiring her audience. Art is not always meant to be pleasing or easily digestible and if we're not prepared to take the time to explore the bizarre beyond its superficial weirdness, we risk missing the point. It's easy to interpret the strange or perplexing as a negative thing and be repelled by it. But could we be 'one of a kind' without it? Could we be distinctive or, hell, *iconic* in our field by playing it safe?

One of the most fascinating things about Lady Gaga - aside from the unparalleled creativity expressed in her costumes and music alike (Google her outfits!) - has been her ability to embrace metamorphosis. After the flop of her album Artpop, she went back to the drawing board. Artpop was the end of Lady Gaga in her debut form. The album has been described as being *"Gaga's nose-dive into her own gaga-ness."*[69]

In 2015, Lauren Duca needled in the Huffington Post:

"Gaga's avant gardism has become as hollow as one of Jeff Koons' balloon animal sculptures."[70]

Jeff Koon is an artist who invented those cartoonish balloon animals you see at children's birthday parties. #ouch

Writing for the Observer in 2018, Helen Holmes said of Lady Gaga:

"Her aesthetic restlessness permeated everything she did, until her thrilling unpredictability reached its inevitable conclusion: It became predictable. Lady Gaga's cacophonous clutter reached its zenith with Artpop, her divisive third studio album..."[71]

Here is one of the most important lessons about being an iconic brand: you must continually evolve. Lady Gaga had outgrown herself. Brands are not (or shouldn't be) static. Brand managers have to navigate a cycle of 'endings and beginnings' and be alert to signs that an upheaval is imminent. Little red flags begin appearing to hint that transformation is on the way.

It's common for my clients to miss the signals while learning how to ride the wave of evolution. While every leader's experience is unique, they'll start noticing things like the client contracts they relied on begin to end, the opportunities that once flowed through start to taper off, successful strategies will stop producing results, and the cogs of relationships and networks which once whirred effortlessly together will start to lock and grind.

Often clients will keep on pursuing the same activities despite feeling perplexed about their lack of efficacy. They become driven by fear - "Why is this ending? Why is this not working?" - instead of turning their attention to, "What's the next step, now?" This tug of war continues until a crisis occurs (like an album flop) that is impossible to ignore.

A client of mine who recently experienced this described her frustration at struggling to find the calibre of business connections she wanted in the circle of leaders she'd networked with for a long time. She said:

"I walked into the room and realised that this is not where I belong anymore."

On this journey, it's common for leaders to up level beyond the networks or ecosystems they once thrived in. You've likely experienced it yourself at some point. If you have a dynamic brand - one that's growing and evolving - it follows that your network also has to be dynamic. And remember, just as you and your brand are constantly changing, so are the businesses and people within your network. Everything is always in a state of flux. You'll outgrow some relationships, you'll have to recalibrate with others, and you'll have to keep replenishing your network with new and exciting contacts.

Did Lady Gaga know the album flop was coming? Possibly. Deep down. Somewhere. But it's equally possible she relied on proven techniques with confidence and was surprised at the result. Does this mean the album was worthless? Absolutely not. It's been said that failure is the mother of innovation.[72] That album signified a pivotal moment in Lady Gaga's career. She likely wouldn't be who she is today without it.

Many of the greatest pioneers in history have gone through a similar cycle. They experiment, fail, succeed, disrupt, experiment, fail, evolve, and succeed again.

Founder and CEO, Mark Randolph, reveals this is exactly what underlies the success of media-service provider and production company Netflix. Described by Lucy Stone in the Brisbane Times:

"Netflix's success wasn't simply a case of a 'eureka moment', with a fully-formed, viable idea appearing from the sky that caused the upheaval of years of technology. He and his co-founders went through hundreds of ideas, testing each one-by-one - many of them bad, he said."[73]

While Netflix and Gaga are entirely different entities, it's all about innovation. The commonalities bleed through industries. Singularity isn't reserved for only Hollywood celebrities or popstars. The means of expressing brand individuality could be a meat dress, or it could be providing a new way to watch television. It's all valid.

Once you've blown the lid off all expectations like Lady Gaga, is there anywhere left to go? Yes! Back inside yourself, of course - and that's exactly what Lady Gaga did. The result is what could only be described as a 'naked' version of Gaga, like a 'naked' wedding cake with only the slightest scraping of frosting. Gone were the wacky threads and accessories and, in their place, was a woman peeled back to her (almost completely natural) core, with long, flowing blonde hair and glowing skin. Having once lampooned her for being 'a manufactured product', critics now began announcing Gaga's career-suicide because she was acting 'normal'!

As Lindsay Zoladz wrote for Vulture in 2015:

"The woman who made pop weird is now playing around with being normal. Or her version of it."

And:

"Lady Gaga is playing a joke on us."[74]

But maybe, just maybe, she wasn't. Maybe she was just ready to become the next edition of herself. In fact, she says:

"I don't think the world was ready to see who I really am because I wasn't ready to be myself. I'm saying: 'This is me with nothing.'"[75]

And:

"I've come to accept that I discovered my beauty by having the ability to invent myself and transform."[76]

I began to wonder how possible it is to completely remodel ourselves as human beings. It's widely accepted we can change our opinions. We've seen ministers of religion transmogrify to outspoken atheists (e.g. former evangelical preacher Dan Barker, now co-president of America's Freedom From Religion Foundation), atheists become devout Christians (e.g. Peter Hitchens, brother of the famous atheist, Christopher Hitchens), Neo-Nazi racists see the error of their ways (e.g. Ken Parker, former KKK member and Neo-Nazi) and radicals become conservative (arguably almost a whole generation of beatniks and hippies who seem to have joined the American 'Tea Party' movement). We can also change habits and manage aspects of our personality. But what about out-and-out change at our core?

Personality can adapt over time, and we can have dramatic changes in response to major life events (including traumatic or 'road to Damascus' ones). According to psychologists Wiebke Bleidorn,

Christopher Hopwood and Richard Lucas, changes to personality due to life events in general are:

"Relatively modest in magnitude and depend on the type of event and the trait."[77]

Mathias Allemand and Christoph Flückiger, psychologists from the University of Zurich, describe a 'hierarchy of changeability.'[78] That is, core parts of our personality will remain stable, other parts may change slightly over a long period of time, while remaining parts can be more unpredictable on a day by day basis. For example, you may generally be a calm person, but, given the right set of conditions, your calm demeanour can go out the window and you have the potential to fly off the handle. It may be a temporary response, and you may be more resilient to a similar circumstance in the future, but fluctuations are possible.

Intentional change is also possible, but it takes hard work and commitment. Specifically:

"... interventions have to target patterns of thoughts, feelings, and behaviors, and not only single, specific attributes of personality."

And

"Only through repeated practice and reinforcement over time, new behaviors and experiences may become learned, habitual and automatized."[79]

In 2014, an American research team headed by psychologist, Dr Benjamin Chapman found:

"The process of habit formation may ultimately impart permanent changes that may be manifested in changes at the trait-level."[80]

While life experiences can influence personality, it also works the other way; personality can predict outcomes. For example, someone who is highly neurotic may be more likely to experience depression or mood disorders.

There are some pre-conditions necessary in order to effect change:

1. Change must either be desirable or necessary.

2. The individual must consider the change to be feasible, i.e. achievable.
3. The steps necessary to make the change must be repeated until they become habitual.

It's important to point out that the intervention itself must be fit for purpose. There are some skills, strategies, approaches, and methods that can be developed with training or coaching. Others, such as mood disorders or mental illness, require medical and therapeutic intervention. Researchers themselves warn there is a lack of empirical evidence to support personality changes as a result of intervention. Then again, studies with good methodologies suggest people can make modest changes and maintain them. Regardless, the research is in its infancy.

With this in mind, it is entirely plausible that we can have or develop seemingly contradictory parts of ourselves that we choose to express or suppress at any given time, while still being who we've always been.

Gaga's next album, Joanne, wasn't a raging success by music chart standards either, but iconic brands need to measure their success beyond the short-term metrics. Artpop and Joanne are beacons, lighting the path for the next incarnation of Gaga, the artist. These transformative albums, exposing the artist's vulnerability, were incredibly risky.

In 2018, Lady Gaga diversified into acting, playing Ally in the movie, A Star is Born. The movie itself asks questions about how we define authenticity: Is a person who dyes their hair, slathers themselves in make-up and layers their body in outrageous costumes, less authentic than one with natural hair and bare skin? No. Lady Gaga is no less real in a meat dress than she is standing completely naked in the shower.

Fittingly, Gaga has launched a new makeup line, Haus Laboratories. A recent Instagram post describes the brand's ethos:

"Our tools were designed with artistry and versatility in mind to inspire endless self-expression and reinvention.'[81]

And on another post, *"There are no rules.'*[82]

While I'm not keen on the meat dress (but appreciate how brave that was), exploring Gaga and her focus on reinvention has been incredibly profound. What matters, and what we can take away from this, is that how Gaga or any of us face the world and express our identity with substance is our truth at that time. Who is anyone to dictate that a person can't live and express themselves in different truths? Who are we to deny an individual growth, or to say they must conform to one category, label, or persona and stick with it, come hell or high water?

For me, writing this book is the culmination of who I once was. A final shedding of armour. A moment of rebirth. I've realised that this incredible process of finding and reinventing myself will be repeated, again and again, over my lifetime. This is no longer the tale of a woman fighting just to be who she is, free from judgement. As Gaga demonstrates, the judgement will always be there. No more dodging myself like I'm some kind of prickly cactus. No more basing my worth and value as a brand on vanity metrics that reinforce conformity. After all, what if the very thing you reject about yourself, or that others have rejected, is the secret ingredient to becoming who you're destined to be?

In her Musicians of Google interview, Gaga emphasised the difference between changing ourselves for others and changing for ourselves. She says:

"I can't tell you how many times I get phone calls from TV stations, and Troy [Carter - Gaga's manager] will call me and he'll say, 'They want you to edit out this section of the video' and I say, 'Well, just tell them I'm not doing it and if they don't want to play it they don't have to.' Because, if the artist is constantly moulding ourselves and changing and abridging what we do for the machine, then the artist becomes part of the machine.'[83]

Lastly, in the same interview she draws attention to the process of finding our diamonds:

"I really encourage people to look into the darkness and look into places you would not normally look to find uniqueness and specialness, because that's where the diamonds are hiding.'[84]

I was quite taken aback hearing this from her. It mirrored the exact process I had been through, right down to describing the experience of finding diamonds in the messiest of places. It was then that I fully accepted for the first time that I was on the right track. Being able to look into our own darkness and find the beauty is the most powerful and courageous thing we can do as leaders. Self-knowledge and self-acceptance are prerequisites for reinvention; self-love is where true leadership power is found. I realised that facing one of the things that I was most afraid of (my own unlikeability) and pulling it apart like splitting hairs, not only changed my view on it, but was incredibly brave. I felt resolute.

SIDE NOTE: For her work on A Star is Born, Lady Gaga was nominated for Best Actress and won the Oscar for Best Original Song at the 2019 Academy Awards - despite the critics.

TASK: How can you create opportunities to achieve success because of your eccentricities rather than despite them?

CHAPTER NINE

Shedding the 'Shoulds'

As leaders, how can we succeed by stepping into the truth of who we are? How can we be ourselves confidently and unapologetically - owning our unique identity?

Everyone is like, "Just be yourself!" and we're like, "Yeah!" But the enthusiasm is often short-lived. This is because such sentiments don't address the underlying barriers that prevent us from 'just being ourselves.' It's like saying to someone, "You should get out of jail" and they say "Yeah!" but unless there's a key involved in this master plan, or they're El Chapo, it's just not going to happen.

What commonly happens when you ask someone who they really are - and who they want to be - is that the 'shoulds' start creeping in. The 'shoulds' are like photoshop tools; we take a selfie which shows who we truly are and edit it to fit what society says we SHOULD be. It's so ingrained we often believe those standards are our own. We adopt them as our own under the guise of 'choice' and 'freedom of thought.' But the 'should' prerequisites prevent us from living the full expression of ourselves.

By trying to fit in with social expectations which have no bearing on how well we do our jobs, we're bowing to 'conditional equality'. We're accepting a deal that says we can only have equal opportunity if we fit some 'cookie cutter' stereotype of who we should be.

Conditional equality gives the illusion that we all have equal rights to participation in a multicultural, free country like Australia. But it's equal rights with strings attached. And the strings are held, very tightly, by the privileged, or 'elite' group that's running the show.

In a broader context, but in the same way, conditional equality is afforded to minority or disadvantaged groups by the mainstream gatekeepers. Essentially, elite or in-groups selectively grant permission for members of out-groups to join the team, provided you 'fit the mould'. If you dare to step outside the lines that have been drawn for you, the gatekeepers maintain the right to irrevocably revoke your membership privileges. In other words: "You have permission to participate as long as you abide by our rules - the rules we made up to protect our status and advance our agenda. As long as you're happy to help with that goal, welcome aboard!" Conditional equality is equality with an awful lot of fine print.

An incredibly inspiring leader, Yassmin Abdel-Magied, hit the nail on the head by arguing that true equality requires no assignment of permission. I had the absolute pleasure of speaking with Yassmin about the topic of unlikeability and structural inequality. She was incredibly generous with her time, wisdom, and insight. Listening to Yassmin speak was a humbling experience. The depth of her resilience is something to be admired.

Yassmin is a Sudanese-Australian, a Muslim, a mechanical engineer, a social activist and a published author. She's a global speaker, a broadcaster and multi-award winner (including being named Queensland Young Australian of the Year in 2015). She's also served on boards and as a corporate ambassador for gender equality. But titles and awards are not adequate to explain the depth of Yassmin's insight, the importance of her work or the breadth of her interests. She is the epitome of diversity in all its beauty.

Yassmin is no stranger to going against the grain. Speaking to executive coach Yana Fry in 2016, she said:

"I've almost found my identity as 'the outsider.' I enjoy being someone who's different, because I think that, if you're a little bit different, you can challenge the preconceived notions... And you don't have to adhere to what is considered 'the norm.' If you're outside 'the norm,' how can you be expected to adhere to it? I think it's almost a

gift to be an outsider... Once you start to realise the power of being an outsider and embracing that, you realise that, actually, you can do so much with it.'[85]

I love this.

Yassmin has also borne the brunt of conditional equality in an incredibly vulnerable, violent, public, unimaginable way, and risen from the ashes of that experience with a sense of stoicism. I'm referring to the way she was essentially forced out of Australia after she posted a Facebook status on Anzac Day. For those unfamiliar with the event, Anzac Day is a day of commemoration for Australian and New Zealand soldiers, to honour the sacrifices they have made, and continue to make, for the freedoms we enjoy. It began as a remembrance for the battle of Gallipoli in 1915 but has since evolved to honour all soldiers who served in military conflicts.

In a 2018 article written for Teen Vogue, Yassmin wrote:

"The phrase Australians use for remembrance is 'Lest We Forget.' I wanted to make my sentiment more inclusive than just those who fought in that war. Who else should we not forget, I thought? So, I posted the following: 'Lest We Forget (Manus, Nauru, Syria, Palestine)."[86]

The reference to Manus and Nauru linked the issues of military conflict to the displaced refugees that the Australian government has indefinitely detained in those locations. Her reference to Syria and Palestine acknowledged other victims of war. What happened next is both terrifying and mind-blowing. There was an unprecedented uproar in response to Yassmin's status. She was, in her words, *"made an example of."*[87] The hatred that Yassmin endured included death threats and other invectives so utterly vile she was forced to move to a new house, and ultimately to another country, out of fear for her own safety. This public lambasting spread like wildfire on social media, but also into traditional media, drawing comments from senior political figures. The outrage continued, even after Yassmin conceded her words had caused offence, deleted the status and issued an unreserved apology.

The world's increasing digital connectedness and the rise of social media has led to a revival of brutal public shaming. Jon Ronson wrote in his book, So You've Been Publicly Shamed,[88] that public shaming ended in the late 1830s. It's been reinvigorated in the form of a *"digital ducking stool."*[89]

In a modern-day reinvention of villagers arriving en masse with tar, feathers, and flaming torches, today's netizens seem to delight in rushing from one Twitterstorm to the next. But as Yassmin pointed out to me, digital activism (or digilantism) is "nuanced"; it's not all bad. Those same social media platforms that facilitate public shaming have also provided an avenue for minority groups to call powerful leaders to account and enabled social change through movements like #MeToo.

In a lot of ways the internet has made it much more difficult for people with privilege to control the narrative. But how public shaming impacts us depends on our social status. Yassmin explained she doesn't "agree with a mob mentality" but that when people in power are called to account, it's very different to when disadvantaged groups have their conditional equality revoked.

For Yassmin and others like her, the shaming went beyond a bit of online backlash and degenerated into a torrent of personal abuse. It was not a reasonable response to a status that didn't land as intended. It dehumanised her. Yassmin said her experience was a harsh penalty for "breaching [her] social contract" - the terms and conditions she's required to live by according to Australian society.

The term 'social contract' resonated strongly with me as I reflected on what I've been learning about privilege and disadvantage and how it relates to unlikeability. Many of the issues we see with unlikeability come about when a leader breaches their social contract. The cost of that transgression varies according to the 'terms' of the transgressor's conditional equality. Members of the elite, as we have seen, often get off with no more than a slap to the back of the hand.

Interestingly, a key aspect of Sudanese culture that was instilled in Yassmin growing up was the concept of "reputation." Reputation, in this context, is based on how you perform in terms of community expectations. It is quite distinct from likeability. Yassmin explained that even if someone doesn't 'like' you, they will 'accept' you if you have a good reputation. This explains why Yassmin believed "so deeply" that if she was a "model minority," if she could prove she was worthy, she would earn the right to equal participation in the system. The heartbreaking reality was that in the moment her permission was revoked, none of her previous achievements mattered. The minute she hit "Post" on that Facebook status, Yassmin's reputation in the system was reset to "zero."

Listening to Yassmin speak, I was reminded of what happened to Adam Goodes. Adam was an elite football player for the AFL's (Australian Football League's) Sydney Swans team. AFL is a game that receives national adoration in Australia. Adam is a proud Aboriginal man. After calling out racism in the stands and on and off the field, Adam was demonised. Jeered and booed every time his fingers touched the ball on the field, he was ultimately driven out of the game in the same way that Yassmin was driven out of the country.

There are two trains of thought concerning the Adam Goodes story: the first (and the view that I support) is that it's racism, the second is that Adam Goodes is unlikeable. Rejecting the first hypothesis, the naysayers cry, "Then why is everyone only booing Adam and not other indigenous players?" Perhaps the reason is that Adam was being penalised for breaching his social contract.

In an article for the ABC, Kate Ashton quoted sports commentator, Charlie King:

"King, a Gurindji man and Order of Australia Medal recipient, said Goodes became a target 'because he had power: he was talented, respected, and proud.'

'This is about Adam Goodes because of the powerful position that he held; we didn't like it, so we booed him, and we wanted to cut him down,' he said."

King continued:

"'I think that deep down, that was the problem with Adam Goodes in the eyes of some people - they didn't like the idea that an Aboriginal person could be powerful, and Adam Goodes was powerful, so they set out to crush him, and they did, they were successful in doing it.'"[90]

King's insight reflects a power dynamic theory Professor Shelby Steele called "challengers" and "bargainers." Steele is a conservative, African American expert on multiculturalism and race relations. As Michael

Safi explains in The Guardian, "bargaining" and "challenging" are techniques employed by African American leaders. He says:

"Bargainers emphasise the 'us', forging an unwritten pact with the white public not to show anger at historical racism, provided the public doesn't hold their race against them. Challengers, such as [Adam] Goodes – and [Michael] Long, in a less confrontational way – don't let the white public off the hook so easily, forcing them, as Goodes put it himself in June, to 'have a conversation.'"[91]

It seems the 'fine print' in Adam Goode's social contract stipulated that if he "bargained" with us, we'd tolerate him. If he "challenged" us - that is, stood up to racism, tried to start a constructive national discussion or expressed his culture on field during the Indigenous Round - we would revoke his permission for equality.

The Indigenous round is a series of football games which highlight Indigenous players. Goode's 'sin', doing a celebratory war dance after kicking a goal, seems perfectly in keeping with an event intended to showcase and celebrate Aboriginal sporting culture and achievement. There is no similar outcry when New Zealand's All Blacks perform the Haka, an accepted and celebrated Maori war dance, before their Rugby matches.

Many of Goode's critics said he shamed a 13-year-old girl for screaming out a racist slur - "Ape!" - during a footy match. But in a post-match interview, Adam clearly absolved the girl of blame. He said:

"... you know, it was a 13-year-old girl, but it's not her fault. She's 13, she's still so innocent. I don't put any blame on her. Unfortunately, it's what she hears, the environment she's grown up in.'[92]

Interestingly, just as Yassmin Abdel-Magied was named Queensland Young Australian of the Year in 2015, Adam was honoured as Australian of the Year in 2014. And like Yassmin, that achievement meant nothing when he breached the social contract for conditional equality and saw his permission to "play on our team" revoked. The fact we would ask and expect people in minority groups to wrestle for and compromise power like this is deeply disturbing.

Yassmin insists that achieving systemic change requires "a broad-based acceptance that things need to change." This echoes so much of what I've learnt about the denial of structural and individual inequalities or, as Yassmin terms it, "a deep defensiveness." It brings home the responsibility that powerful and privileged groups have to open doors for change. As individuals, it reminds us to check our privilege, examine our own prejudices, and accept that no change to the status quo comes without some discomfort to the privileged group.

In terms of how her shocking experience laid the groundwork for the next phase of her activism, Yassmin said it was "clarifying" in that it "laid bare how the world works in undeniable terms." It revealed the "double standards" and "hypocrisy." Yassmin said it was "so public, so obliterating" that no one could deny it happened. She said that in 2017, while suffering from isolation and a sense of "complete betrayal," she began a process of detachment from the people and symbols of success she once relied on to define her worth. For example, she stopped looking for validation through awards and nominations because, in the moment where it really counted, the credibility they afforded her meant nothing. Through this process of introspection Yassmin stepped into her leadership power; at that moment she no longer needed outside validation to define her value.

What happened to Yassmin Abdel-Magied is forever etched in the public record through such an extensive digital trail that it's enabled her to speak globally about her experience and utilise it to pursue change for the better. No one can argue that it didn't happen.

In everything I've read and heard from Yassmin, I see a leader who has gone through the process of shedding her 'shoulds.' It's a process I've mirrored in my own journey, and one that's essential to coming to the truth of who we are. The drafting of these unspoken rules of inclusion and exclusion is complex and steeped in history. The reinforcement of them is ongoing, even in subtle ways. What role could we all be playing in upholding them?

Asking you to find and embrace the truth of who you really are is not just some empty, motivational slogan designed to hype you up so you can sell more 'widgets.' It's not about affecting false confidence and a 'positive attitude.' Remember, I'm the "anti-guru." This goes beyond business and leadership; it's learning how to "be." It's about living that authentic expression of ourselves every day, discarding the 'shoulds' and shedding that old, people-pleasing skin. It's about finding the unique parts of ourselves that we need to polish and letting them shine. The way to effect change is to model that change; to BE the future you want to see. And a great start is to tear up that social contract - whether we're the party offering it or signing it. Let's stop making equality conditional and celebrate the amazing benefits diversity brings to the business world, the sporting world, and the world in general.

Yassmin's story demonstrates that shedding our 'shoulds' is not always easy or straightforward and the journey is not always perfect. Some 'shoulds' will take longer than others. Some will be excised cleanly; others will require deeper cuts and considerably more pain. Some will creep back and turn up on our doorstep long after we thought they had moved on. Some changes will be well received, and others will take time, perhaps years, before gaining acceptance. No matter what happens, doing an Elsa and letting go of our 'shoulds' plays a significant role in our personal growth as leaders and as humans. Each step forward without a 'should' is a step towards your individual power.

What advice would Yassmin give to members of minority groups who are afraid to step out into the spotlight?

She says, firstly, be prepared for the heat. But secondly, don't tackle your haters head-on and fight alone. Instead, she recommends forming a coalition or cabinet of allies who can help you create a parallel system for responding strategically. For example, she suggests not responding to biased media reports directly, but finding allies in the media who will share another side to the story. Yassmin is now very careful about where and how she spends her time and energy. She focuses on work that will progress her movement forward. Highlighting the need for self-care, she also refuses to subject herself to spaces that are not safe for her. In the quest to achieve diversity, no one should feel pressured to engage in debates or dialogue that are disrespectful or work within spaces that are harmful to their wellbeing.

This was a 'lightbulb' moment for me. I worried that, moving forward, being selective about the spaces I engage in meant closing myself off to diversity, and that that was a bad thing. I worried that by heeding my 'gut instinct' and avoiding spaces that made me uncomfortable, I was being less accepting of people or groups with different values or points of view. It brought to the surface a 'should' of my own: that I was somehow required to participate indiscriminately in all expressions of diversity, regardless of the personal cost. Yassmin was quite rightfully resolute that no one is required to engage in a space that is, or feels, unsafe for them.

If Yassmin Abdel-Magied can provide any inspiration to current and future generations of leaders, it is in the way she not only survived, but emerged triumphant from such a ghastly experience. While some may not fully appreciate the impact of her work now, Yassmin encourages us to reflect on the dark aspects of our national history, as well as our modern-day perpetuation of inequality. She is breaking down barriers by calling out assumptions. Yassmin is a shining example of how even intense 'unlikeability' can be galvanised to work for you. That moment of Yassmin stepping into her power after being nationally vilified, ironically provided her with a global platform to advance her cause.

Speaking to Yassmin, I felt her inner power - it emanated from her. Like Nelson Mandela, Yassmin experienced deep pain, torment, and rejection but emerged arguing, not for vengeance, but for peace, understanding, diversity, and tolerance. I strongly suspect that Yassmin will continue to grow in her leadership and global prominence and that, in the decades (maybe even centuries) to come, Australians will both recognise and regret what she went through, and be grateful she had the bravery to continue on, for the benefit of all of us.

TASKS:

1. Write down all the 'shoulds' you're ready to shed and make clear commitments about how you are going to shed them.

2. Ask yourself, "What's the best thing about being an outsider?"

3. Build your coalition or cabinet for safety and support and for devising and implementing parallel strategies.

_____

_____

_____

_____

_____

_____

_____

_____

_____

_____

_____

_____

'Toot Sweet' Recap:

1. Accepting and harnessing your unique mind will enable you to live your genius.

2. Your authentic self can evolve over a lifetime and you make the rules.

3. Create a cabinet of trusted allies who can help you circumvent the system.

CHAPTER TEN

The Grand Slam of Unlikeability

Serena Williams' is the kind of success story that divides rooms.

She will probably divide the readers of this book, too. In full transparency, I resisted writing about Serena, though I couldn't quite put my finger on why I was reluctant to include her. After all, I was, and still am, a strong supporter of her as a diverse leader. So why, sweet Moses on a push bike, was I having this 'dancing on hot coals' moment about putting her in my book?

By this point in the writing process I had become well versed in exploring resistances. I knew I was about to learn something about myself through Serena. I realised if I didn't write about her I'd be betraying the entire message of this book; to have the courage to look at all your 'icky', 'unlikeable' bits, bring them into the light, and decide whether to discard them or polish them up like diamonds. It was a very vulnerable moment: a "What's the point of this project anyway?" moment. I have to admit I threw a little internal tantrum out of frustration at myself.

Let's break cake.

For me, the sticking point in writing about Serena Williams as a leader to admire and emulate was the on-court incident where she threatened to shove a tennis ball down a female line umpire's throat. Now, without a doubt, this isn't dissimilar to other on-court meltdowns from other tennis greats. Tennis players have probably been having meltdowns since the French, shouting *"Tenez!"* ("Play!"), first started thwacking a ball back and forth with the palms of their hands. It's a fair call to say tennis is an aggressive, hostile sport. Do I think it's reasonable to expect elite tennis players and athletes to control their emotions in the heat of battle? Yes. Of course, I say that with no experience of what being a professional under that kind of intense pressure is like. But is 'working under pressure' a 'get out of jail free' card for telling people you're going to shove a ball into their oesophagus?

Frankly, I was disappointed in Serena. I thought she was a better person. I felt she'd failed in her responsibility as a role model. I was torn in my admiration of her. If I included her in my book, if I accepted this unlikeable part of how tennis players conduct themselves, was I condoning it? Ah! There was the resistance in all its glory. Determined, I pressed on.

Serena is, without any doubt, the number one female tennis player in the world. What she lacks in agility, she makes up in power and strategy. She is a force to be reckoned with, both on and off the court. I love it, but, for some, it can be difficult to digest. She's been labelled everything from inspirational to downright arrogant. At first, we wonder, "Where there's smoke, is there fire? Is all, or any, of the negative chatter about Serena true?" As I began to research these questions, I started to realise I'd been looking at Serena's 'unlikeability' from a very superficial perspective.

In the likeability stakes, Serena Williams not only faces one or two personal disadvantages, but at least 11, all together and all at once.

- She is a woman.
- She is a hugely successful woman.
- She is a woman approaching middle-age.
- She's physically powerful and therefore seen as 'unfeminine.'
- She is confident and outspoken.
- She self-promotes.

- She is a feminist.
- She also holds some conservative views.
- She's a mother.
- She proactively channels anger into her deadly tennis game (on the advice of her coach).
- She is a woman of colour.

Refusing to be self-deprecating or meek - qualities we typically associate with 'good' women - Serena Williams wins the Grand Slam of unlikeability. As she is an anomaly, people are unsure how to take her; they struggle to put her into a box or sort her into a category, and that makes them feel uncomfortable.

Despite her undeniable talent and success, Serena Williams earns less in endorsements than other female athletes who fit stereotypical norms. In 2013, Stephen Rodrick, writing for Rolling Stone, explained:

"Here are the facts. Serena is the number-one tennis player in the world. Maria Sharapova is the number-two tennis player in the world. Sharapova is tall, white and blond, and because of that, makes more money in endorsements than Serena, who is black, beautiful and built like one of those monster trucks that crushes Volkswagens at sports arenas. Sharapova has not beaten Serena in nine years. Think about that for a moment."[93]

At times Serena has been the subject of outright ridicule. As Ben Rothenburg said in The New York Times in 2015:

"Over the years, Williams has been described by online commenters and journalists alike as a 'gorilla,' as 'manly' and as 'savage.'"[94]

Rothenburg describes how other tennis players have ridiculed Serena by imitating her appearance and concludes:

"On the surface, it may look like playful athletic ribbing, but these kind of incidents, coupled with the language so often used to describe Serena as an athlete, speak to a kind of dehumanization specific to black women. As Ms. Magazine writer Corinne Gaston puts it, the policing of Williams' body 'comes gift-wrapped in a triad from hell: misogyny, racism and transphobia.'"[95]

Head in hands at my laptop, tears welled up and ran towards the keyboard. I felt incredible pain trying to understand what this constant barrage of backlash and ridicule must be like. Some might say, "Well that's your job. You put yourself in the spotlight, so you have to live with it." But why? Why should anyone have to live with it? It sounds like a poor excuse to justify harmful and hateful commentary as reasonable discourse. Discrimination and abuse as part and parcel of a legitimate career choice? I'm not swallowing that.

How does anyone cope with this existence, day in, day out, and still perform to Serena's standard?

Stephen Rodrick in Rolling Stone, in 2013, explains:

"Serena's dominance has been fuelled by not giving a shit what you or anyone else thinks about her methods."[96]

And further, that she simply wouldn't give *"a flying fuck what you thought."*[97]

I'm sure on some level Serena does care. I mean, I haven't personally asked her, but even those of us who have shielded our hearts in armour sometimes feel the sting of a well-aimed poison arrow. But perhaps what Stephen Rodrick is referring to isn't that Serena doesn't point blank not care but, resiliently, she's found a way to use that emotion to her own advantage. The difference is subtle but powerful.

Having no emotional response to a constant barrage of criticism would be psychopathic. Choosing how you filter and utilise that natural response is damn smart and hugely empowering. Here's an example to illustrate. A person might not care about someone's transphobic abuse towards them, because they recognise that the vilification is a reflection of the abuser and says nothing about their own value and dignity as a person. However, they might care that this kind of abuse exists and that it prevents people like them from having basic human rights. If they are a leader in this space, they will care enough to stand up to it but not in a way that reduces them to arguing with idiots. It's about making a point of leading by example, by channelling their response to abuse into their work in a positive way that paves the way for human rights. So, it's not that someone doesn't care about abuse, it's that they turn it into a positive by channelling their response to it into everything they do; whether directly or indirectly.

Serena has spoken about her difficulties with body image and how she is helping women of all shapes and sizes to redefine beauty. She's not ashamed of her body. More than that, she celebrates its beauty. She is challenging the bullshit idea that all women should look a certain way. We see this echoed in her "Serena" clothing line, with outfits designed to fit all different body shapes, and the use of diverse models, including women with disabilities. In other words, Serena has set up personal boundaries and she's standing powerfully within them, defending her turf. That can rattle the cages of many people.

It was now that I realised something powerful had happened.

When I went out into my market and started talking about the personal criticism I received and that I was exploring the potential power of being 'unlikeable,' something very strange occurred. All of a sudden, the negative feedback stopped. It was "crickets." Soon after I made the very first, tentative steps towards claiming my 'unlikeability,' I realised that now there was only positive feedback flowing towards me.

I mentioned this to my mentor and asked him if he could explain it. He said, "You've typed Google into Google and blown up the internet."

I laughed.

What on earth was going on?

Enter Sarah Blake, an award-winning conflict resolution strategist. I called her and asked if she could explain this development. Sarah immediately recognised the unfolding pattern and assured me this was common. She called it 'power shifts.' Sarah explained:

"When people are trying to resolve conflict we often see shifts and movement of power. For instance, when we re-establish our boundaries, it doesn't just impact us, but those around us. It is a power shift when we no longer care about what 'they' bring to flame of conflict. Our boundaries mean we no longer bite back.

For people who are insecure, they take this change personally, often because the conflict itself gave them purpose and a sense of connection. When you re-establish your boundary, you'll notice that they will change tactics - they'll keep coming back seeking validation, testing, testing, testing, trying to gain back the control and influence that they need to feel validated. Resist. Eventually, they let go.

When you went out into the market and said, 'I know I'm not for everyone and I'm okay with that,' and 'I'm unlikeable and that's a strength,' you gave them the power to make an informed decision about opting in or out. But you also recreated a power shift that is self-contained, resilient and clear."

Now, I'm not dealing with the level of backlash that Serena experiences but I could see similarities in holding our power. That's not to say the backlash against me might not start again - or increase as my brand grows. But what's shifted and changed is that now I know how to deal with it through maintaining my power. I still care that people find me unlikeable but the way I care is different. There's an acceptance and a focus on channelling my efforts to help others feel free to live their individual identities. This book is an example of that.

Does this mean we can live in blissful ignorance about what our critics are saying? Absolutely not. Being aware of what they're saying and the positions they're taking helps us to shape our campaigns, whether those are business campaigns or social movements. Strategically responding to critics can be valuable for clarifying and honing your message.

SIDE NOTE: I just said critics were a good thing rather than a thorn in our side. Ha! Wonders never cease.

I can't write a chapter about Serena and not address her on-court behaviour. Yes, we're back at the ball in the gullet thing that's been sticking in *my* craw.

Backlash against Serena hit fever-pitch in 2017 when umpire Carlos Ramos issued three code violations, costing her the game against Naomi Osaka. The first violation was for receiving 'coaching' during the game from her coach, Patrick Mouratoglou. The second was for smashing her racket in exasperation over a close line call. Serena argued with Ramos that she wasn't receiving coaching and he issued a third violation for arguing and calling him a "thief." In the ensuing discussion, many, including Serena's own coach, have pointed out the penalties against her were unfair, racist and misogynistic.

Mouratoglou supported Serena by saying:

"... I'm honest, I was coaching. I mean, I don't think she looked at me, so that's why she didn't even think I was. I was like 100 percent of the coaches on 100 percent of the matches, so we have to stop this hypocrite thing. Sascha [Bajin, Osaka's coach,] was coaching every point, too. This chair umpire was the chair umpire of most of the finals of Rafa [Nadal], and Toni's [Rafa's uncle] coaching every single point, and they never gave a warning. I don't really get it. It's strange."[98]

Sportswriter Jerry Bembry wrote in The Undefeated in 2018 that Serena's meltdown deserved criticism but:

"Novak Djokovic, who won the 2018 US Open on Sunday, had to issue a video apology after an aggressive gesture startled a ball boy working the championship match of the 2015 Miami Open.

Nick Kyrgios, from Australia, has earned his bad-boy reputation berating officials, smashing rackets and even appearing to cheat the game by seemingly tanking matches.

And we've all heard about or seen the childish behavior demonstrated by John McEnroe throughout his 16-year career. In 1990, McEnroe was actually defaulted out in the fourth round of the Australian Open for a prolonged tantrum that was mild by his standards, explaining years later, 'I suppose that even though I don't feel like I should have been defaulted, say, in that particular match, I'm sure there were a few others where I probably deserved to be.'"[99]

Bembry continues:

"... male athletes in tennis are judged by a different criteria from their female counterparts. Their actions are embraced as passion, and often applauded. Williams and the other women on tour - especially women of color - have to be twice as good and half as mad to succeed. It's a criteria they have to navigate in tennis, and in life. Women have to work harder because their work often falls under more scrutiny."[100]

As Elizabeth Kiefer at Girlboss says:

"... Andy Murray kicking a tennis ball at an umpire's head during the Cincinnati Masters tournament in 2016, Jimmy Connors yelling at umpire David Littlefield during the 1991 US Open - and at one point, calling him, confusingly, an 'abortion,' and Andy Roddick swearing at the umpire, as well as calling the

officiating into question, during the 2010 US open… It bears mentioning that in those three examples, none of the men were penalized, despite behavior that was as fiery as Williams' was."[101]

What's not in dispute is that these examples aren't exemplary professional behaviour. You know, like, we can't walk into work and threaten to shove a laptop down someone's throat. But in many ways (whether we agree with it or not) it's become an accepted practice in tennis. The problem is it's more accepted for some than for others. As George Orwell wrote in Animal Farm:

"All animals are equal, but some animals are more equal than others."[102]

If we want to address bad behaviour we need to do so across the board, not for a select few whose equality is conditional.

Serena took the fall for equality this time. She said it *"didn't work out"* on this occasion, but she hopes that through her actions it will work out for the next person.[103] And that, dear Unlikeables, is where it all came full circle in the Serena chapter. She ran the gauntlet to show other women and women of colour that there was a way through. She could have said nothing and done nothing, protected her 'likeability' and left the discrimination unchallenged. But she didn't. She stood up. If that kind of sacrifice isn't being the 'better person,' then what is? It's a sacrifice we must acknowledge.

Serena has millions of fans around the world who, rather than being intimidated by her, see themselves in her. She inspires them, is admired by them, and she fights for them. Even though we are different people who face different obstacles, I see parts of myself in her too. I feel Serena Williams' inner flame and honour her bravery to fight for what she believes in.

TASK: Get clear on defining your personal boundaries.

CHAPTER ELEVEN

The Link

Upon reaching this point in the unlikeability journey, I felt enriched and certain that unlikeability plays a positive role in our leadership performance.

I knew a lot more about the fundamentals of what makes us 'unlikeable.' I'd explored how people like Yassmin Abdel-Magied and Serena Williams faced a barrage of hostility but learned to channel their 'unlikeability' for their own (and others') benefit. And I'd uncovered powerful examples of leaders like Amy Winehouse and Lady Gaga who stepped into their unlikeability to become global icons. For the first time, I felt like being unlikeable was an honour. I discovered that embracing my unlikeability made me likeable in an authentic way, without throwing up barriers to effective leadership. I also realised that embracing my unlikeability and being at peace with it was powerful.

A feeling of freedom and love landed in my chest cavity, like a bird soaring in after an epic migration. I felt my heart swell as these new sensations suffused my body, taking up residence in the welcoming nest I'd been preparing for them. All the barbs of unlikeability had been removed from my flesh and I had begun to heal. It's not that I wasn't loved before but this was the moment I truly began to see, hear and feel it. The love was there all along but I wasn't really open to receiving it. I'd been so busy worrying about the people who didn't like me, I hadn't fully appreciated all the love that was coming my way. I'd been so worried that people wouldn't love me if they really knew me, I hadn't stopped to consider that people might love me because, not in spite, of my 'faults.' Never had I thought that unlikeability and love could exist in the same sentence, concept, or thought. But here we are.

Expanding on that theme, when we think about the most loved leaders to walk the earth, how has unlikeability played into their story? Arguably, we can't go past Princess Diana as one of the most loved public figures in history. Yet, Diana's struggle in coming to terms with her own identity played out on an international stage.

When Diana was first introduced to the world, she seemed to have all the attributes of the perfect Princess. She was from an aristocratic family, a virgin, white, and glamorous, yet she appeared shy and demure. We quickly learned, however, that Diana was far more than she seemed; this shy kindergarten teacher would change everything.

From the beginning, it was clear Diana was going to do things differently. She didn't promise to obey her husband in her wedding vows, she sent her children to a regular day school, and she tried to give them a semblance of an 'ordinary' life. She showed emotion in public, and was openly affectionate with her boys, Princes William and Harry. Bucking tradition, Diana didn't wear gloves when meeting members of the public, famously shaking the hands of HIV sufferers bare handed. This simple act was momentous for educating people that HIV/AIDS was not easily transmissible and in breaking down the stigma that surrounded the disease. The royal chef also spoke of how Diana unexpectedly went into the kitchen, made him a cup of tea and thanked staff for the delicious dinners they cooked.[104] She used her immense fame for good, giving her patronage and active involvement to many charitable causes. Diana reinvented the role of being a princess and, in a lot of ways, changed and modernised the institution of British royalty.

To the outside world, Diana seemed like a deeply complex character - very insecure, if not a little neurotic. Behind the glitz and glamour of it all, she suffered incredible loneliness. Already scarred by her parents' messy and very public divorce, Diana faced many more challenges as a young woman thrust into the public spotlight: international fame and unprecedented media scrutiny, the paparazzi, the labyrinthine and often catty politics of the Royal Court, childbirth and motherhood, Prince Charles' affair with Camilla, and a disintegrating marriage. No wonder she struggled with bulimia, depression, and even suicidal ideation.

It's an existence that most of us will never fully understand, though we all watched the carnage with a combination of fascination and horror. The interest in Diana was unfathomable, and perhaps will always be so. She came at a time when many felt alienated by the royal family. Despite her personal battles, Diana single-handedly restored public affection for, and interest in, an institution that had become fusty, remote and irrelevant.

I tried many times to delve into Diana, to really understand what made her tick, and yet, the deeper I went, the more perplexing I found her. Then I realised that her complexity is what people loved about her. Dubbed 'the People's Princess', her brand was built on her imperfect nature. Diana's fans saw her as one of them, and saw their own experiences reflected in hers. As a mother, a wife scorned, a woman reclaiming her life post-divorce, a person working to do good in the community, Diana humanised the Royal Family. She wasn't distant and remote; you could see every thought she had writ large on that expressive face, and people identified with her personal struggles. But still, her position, her title, her fame, her extraordinary beauty, and her charisma elevated her and set her apart. As close as people felt to Diana, she seemed more like the goddess she was named for than one of us mere mortals. And then, Diana was killed in a car accident in Paris while being chased by paparazzi. The impact of this undeniable proof of her mortality shook the world.

Diana

Royalty

Mortal

Human

At her funeral, Diana's brother, Earl Spencer, refused to mince words when describing her life:

"It is a point to remember, that of all the ironies about Diana, perhaps the greatest was this: a girl given the name of the ancient Goddess of hunting was, in the end, the most hunted person of the modern age."[105]

Earl Spencer was, of course, referring to the media pack that went to extraordinary lengths to hunt down the most 'wanted' woman in the world and claim the bounty - a photograph of Diana sold to the highest bidder. It was blood-thirsty work.

The public were understandably heartbroken and angry, but also had to face difficult questions about how complicit we were in the outcome, given our endless obsession with the princess. After all, we eagerly bought the newspapers and magazines that paid the stalkers, didn't we? Granted, many of us didn't understand the extent of our role in the relentless pursuit of the princess but hindsight tragically gives us 20/20 vision.

Princess Diana's death changed many things about how royalty and the general public interact, particularly through the media. In the UK, new lines were drawn legislatively between public and private lives. While the Protection Against Harassment Act was introduced just prior to Diana's death, the editorial code of practice was revised because of it. Lessons learned in the wake of Diana's death have enabled public figures to make more empowered choices about their public and private lives although, for Diana, those changes came too late.

A woman so loved, so revered, would surely not face issues with unlikeability, right?

Spectacularly wrong, Toto.

Despite all the public adoration, Diana has had her fair share of critics, in both life and death. Some of the posthumous evaluations of Diana seemed to revel in speaking ill of the dead.

While Hilary Mantel insists she wasn't criticising Diana, she wrote for The Guardian in 2017:

"They [the pre-recorded tapes for the documentary, Diana in her Own Words] were trailed as revealing a princess who is 'candid' and 'uninhibited.' Yet never has she appeared so self-conscious and recalcitrant. Squirming, twitching, avoiding the camera's eye, she describes herself hopefully as "a rebel", on the grounds that she liked to do the opposite of everyone else. You want to veil the lens and explain: that is reaction, not rebellion. Throwing a tantrum when thwarted doesn't make you a free spirit. Rolling your eyes and shrugging doesn't prove you are brave..."[106]

Mantel went on to propose that we could never truly know Diana, that her brand was like a figment of our imagination; constructed to create an illusion of who we wanted her to be, as opposed to who she really was.

In the New York Post, Maureen Callahan describes how Diana crafted her story 'assiduously.' Echoing Mantel's contention that what the world loved was a 'brand,' and not a real woman, Callahan contends that Diana was a brand myth.[107]

Now, the idea of a 'brand myth' is quite valid. Not only for Diana, but for anyone building a brand. When we think about what we've learnt about how we put together a picture to present to the world, all brands are like myths. Even the way we present ourselves to our neighbours, on social media, to our parents, our clients, our doctor - all of those roles we play in different parts of our lives are also myths. Does this erode the truth, legitimacy or worth of those aspects of ourselves - our personal 'brands'? Absolutely not. It simply shows that everybody has a 'brand.'

Nobody shows all of themselves all the time. Sometimes, depending on the audience, we polish up certain parts of our personality and hide other aspects in the 'bottom drawer.' And it's true that sometimes, with public figures (or even with close acquaintances), we have an inkling about what's in that bottom drawer but because it doesn't mesh with what we want them to be, we turn a blind eye and fall for the 'branding.' But this doesn't make brand strategy akin to forgery.

How possible is it to get a true and complete picture of an individual?

Employing our critical thinking skills and seeking evidence and facts will get us closer to the truth than otherwise possible, but we still can't be certain we've uncovered the ultimate truth. As we've already learned, there is no 'ultimate truth' that can be reflected in a brand. People's lives are dynamic, not static. We change according to context, and we change over time. We are natural chameleons but the fact we show different colours doesn't mean we are hiding our true selves.

A public figure isn't necessarily being deceptive or inauthentic when they don't air all their dirty linen in public. Public figures aren't public property, and nor are we. Honouring your right to privacy does not necessarily make you dishonest. It simply means you are selective about the parts of you that are for sharing, and the parts of you that are reserved for your intimate and personal relationships. Yes, this requires us to be strategic about how we craft our brand in the marketplace. Again, that doesn't suggest we're being disingenuous. We're being purposeful.

The lines were undoubtedly blurred for Diana during her royal life and that intensified her public persona. She was in some ways quite astute and, in other ways, she was making it up as she navigated uncharted waters. Aren't we all doing the same?

Just as being judicious about how we present ourselves publicly isn't necessarily deceptive, the presence of contradictory characteristics isn't evidence of mythmaking. Diana was shy, yet could hold a spotlight or the collective gaze of a room like no one else. She was fiercely brave, yet deeply insecure. Although softly spoken and transparently fragile, she refused to go down without a fight. She was both a heroine and a lamb to the slaughter. In a lot of ways, Diana met the stereotypical rules of being a 'good' woman whilst breaking many others. Her unique blend of qualities led to suggestions that, perhaps, she was not being genuine. How can a person be this and that? Well, they can.

SIDE NOTE: What could have become of Princess Diana if she had broken more rules than she followed?

Yes. Princess Diana had faults - many of them - but her faults made her who she was. People saw in Diana what they wanted to see. It wasn't so much what Diana chose to show or to hide that accounts for the different ways she was perceived, but rather, the different ways people chose to see her. Some looked at Diana, saw only her faults, and dismissed her as a rich, frivolous, dim-witted waste of space. Others saw only her virtues and revered her as a saint. But Diana's 'ideal market' saw both her strengths and weaknesses and recognised that the two were inextricably linked. They loved and admired her because she presented as a real and complex person doing her best under extreme circumstances. The public may not have known all there was to know about Diana but they saw enough to make a judicious assessment that she was a force for good.

If a person like Diana couldn't escape the vice-like grip of unlikeability, then who amongst us can? We can't control how people are going to react to us. As Taylor Swift reminds us, *"Haters gonna hate."*[108] And if we can't control their reactions, why do we let them control us?

We're all inherently likeable and unlikeable to different people, at different times, for various reasons. Further than that, perhaps we NEED to be. What if unlikeability is, in fact, a prerequisite for going against the grain, rebelling, disrupting, and forging new ways forward? Has anyone ever challenged the status quo and not been disliked? Regardless of whether we're changing entire industries, leading and developing teams, or exhibiting personal leadership in a project, if we're not prepared to be unlikeable we're unlikely to get the result we're after.

Being able to shrug off the bogeyman of unlikeability gives us the courage to put forward the crazy idea that changes everything, have a red hot go and test an innovative product, have the hard conversation, or ask an uncomfortable question. Behind every brilliant human innovation stands someone who was prepared to be unlikeable.

If you weren't worried about being likeable, what could you achieve?

We'll never know what could have become of Diana if she had been given the opportunity to live out her life. I'm not sure what I think about the afterlife but if there is one, I hope she knows she was loved and that, despite her feelings of deep inadequacy, she knows she changed the world for the better. Princess Diana was exactly who she was meant to be and needed to be at that point in history. She did the best she could with the resources available to her.

Thinking about Princess Diana made me think about the vicissitudes of my own life; my proudest moments and my deepest regrets. In a lot of ways, Diana reflects our common experience as young and naive adolescents, stumbling along, trying to find our feet. Of course, for some of us that adolescence is more protracted than others, and we're well into adulthood before we start to power forward, confident and surefooted. Some of those life-lessons are incredibly painful, and others joyous, but who would I have become if not for each of them? If the course of history had been different, would I be the same? Would any of us be?

As the character Pip says in Charles Dickens' Great Expectations:

"That was a memorable day to me, for it made great changes in me. But it is the same with any life. Imagine one selected day struck out of it, and think how different its course would have been. Pause you who read this, and think for a moment of the long chain of iron or gold, of thorns or flowers, that would never have bound you, but for the formation of the first link on one memorable day."[109]

Each aspect of Diana's character linked to the next. Each moment in Diana's life linked to the next too. Diana herself is a link in the history of the Royal Family. Regardless of whether we're a princess, or an ordinary Joe sitting at the bus stop, we're creating chains.

Much like Yassmin Abdel-Magied sees being an outsider as a gift and Lady Gaga has mastered evolution, our links are a gift too, preparing us for the next phase. They are testament that our imperfection has purpose. Instead of judging ourselves, can we sit back and accept that we were who we needed to be in that moment? That we are who we are meant to be now? And that we will be who we are meant to be in the future, too? Trusting that each version of ourselves, each link, is leading to something greater, enables us to acknowledge our mistakes, value our imperfections and be empowered to grow - in spite of our critics.

TASK: Consider how each moment in your life journey has contributed to who you have become. Would you be who you are without them?

Despite, or perhaps because of, the hard times, what gifts have these experiences given you?

CHAPTER TWELVE

Becoming an Icon

Is becoming an icon a conscious task or is it an organic by-product of being distinctive in your field?

I asked one of my clients, "Why do you want to be the go-to personal brand in your industry?"

"I want the status," she replied.

The common narrative we hear from leaders, or about leaders, is that they're not in it for the status or fame - that they care about the markets they serve, and that fame is just an organic by-product of that altruistic mission. We love the idea that, one day, a leader just tripped over and accidentally became Oprah. The myth that people accidentally stumble upon status and fame tends to demonise people who have aimed for it, worked hard for it and, yes, even strategized to get it. It sets up a false dichotomy: you either have to care selflessly about your market or care about yourself. It suggests that wanting status or fame is akin to being egotistical; more in it for yourself than anyone else. The truth is, it's not always a zero-sum game.

I then asked this leader, "What does the status give you?"

She responded, "Credibility. A reward for all my hard work helping others."

I love this.

We work damn hard for our successes; we deserve to enjoy the benefits they bring. The irony in the original question is that we can't achieve iconic success without aiming for it. Becoming an icon takes conscious discipline and an unrelenting commitment to excellence. Regardless of whether a person specifically aspires to become 'iconic' (a symbol of excellence and innovation in their field), it remains true that to reach an iconic level of success requires conscious effort.

It's easy to see someone who has reached iconic status and think how lucky they are, how great it must be, and how much fun they must have. What's often not considered is what they went through to get there (and what they go through to stay there). For example, imagine being paid a million dollars just to turn up to a party. Sounds great, right? Imagine becoming the product, where you literally sell your presence and strangers mob you relentlessly for selfies? Sounds much less great, right? Or maybe you wouldn't mind? Now imagine not being able to go anywhere on any given day without security in tow, while you're swarmed by awaiting crowds or assailed by the flashes and clicks of a wall of cameras. Hmmmm. Now of course no job is perfect, and being iconic goes beyond celebrity. But we love to look at all the glitter without thinking about the gristle underneath.

We often look at life - and branding - as a 'double-edged sword.' And, it's true, there are commonly two sides to any success story. But have you ever considered what a double-edged sword is? It's a double-*bladed* sword. It might be harder to use, but a double-edged sword gives the person wielding it an advantage - they have twice the cutting edge and a weapon that cuts on both backward and forward thrusts. This is what we've been learning: while that other 'edge' might seem negative, even dangerous - something we're tempted to grind back and dull down - that second edge is part of our arsenal. If we can learn to wield that double-edged sword, using the 'upside' and the 'downside' in concert, we can attack life with the mastery of Inigo Montoya.

Being iconic is about having an impact on the history of the world in a way that changes how we do things, how we see ourselves or how we understand concepts. Some may argue that being iconic is not always a good thing. Take for example, Hitler, who represents the worst of humanity. Technically, he might meet the definition of an iconic villain, but he isn't iconic - not for the purposes of this discussion. Within the context of this book, becoming an iconic leader or brand is about utilising your unique qualities to make the kind of positive contribution to your field that will be appreciated and remembered for generations.

Contrary to how many of us imagine our lives as an iconic leader might be, there are times when iconic contributions aren't recognised or appreciated until after a person retires, or until well after their death. We wouldn't be using computers today if it wasn't for British scientist Alan Turing, whose iconic contribution to computer science was suppressed, largely due to his homosexuality. It's only recently, and largely due to a Hollywood movie, that African American mathematician Katherine Johnson has been elevated to iconic status for her contribution to the success of the first moon landing. Happily, unlike Turing, Katherine Johnson lived to see her work recognised, but many don't.

One might wonder, 'if we're not going to reap the rewards in our lifetime, what's the point?' Well, it all comes down to how we define 'rewards.' Icons are quite often before their time - they're throwing out new ideas, challenging stereotypes, bucking the system, trying to change the status quo. In fact, in their own time, they're often being downright unlikeable and working against entrenched opposition and prejudice. But a true icon is indefatigable; they will continue toiling, through thick and thin, until the world can't ignore them anymore. They understand that the results don't begin and end with them. They'll work a lifetime, knowing full well that everything they contribute today will change something tomorrow - and that's reward enough.

When thinking about timeless icons, it's hard to go past Freddie Mercury of the iconic British rock band, Queen. Speaking after Freddie's untimely death, Queen's drummer, Roger Taylor, said:

"No one got inside his shell."

"He was quite a mystery."

"He was so much his own creation."[10]

That last comment about being your own creation perfectly encapsulates everything we've discussed. Every leader we've explored together has, in one way or another, been the object of their own creation; their own work of art - the lived version of their own truth. The mystery of Freddie Mercury was part of what made him iconic. He didn't feel he had to make sense to anyone but himself. Freddie's decision not to conform physically, sexually or artistically to society's expectations, but to just be himself, created a unique, mysterious, intriguing, charismatic star whose legend will outlive us all.

Born as Farrokh Bulsara in Zanzibar and nicknamed "Freddie" Freddie Mercury was unapologetically out of sync with his own social and historical context. He was bisexual at a time when homosexuality was still taboo. He was a Parsee Indian at a time when extreme racism and anti-immigration sentiment was rampant in the UK. He had buck teeth. In a country in the grip of Thatcherite conservatism, Freddie took flamboyancy to another level. He loved ballet and rock music simultaneously. And he died of AIDS at a time when the victims of that disease were treated like lepers. Freddie Mercury and Queen did things with rock music that had never been done before. To top it all off, the outrageous extrovert we saw on stage kept his private life strictly private - much to the dismay of the media. Taylor described him as a *"tremendous force of a personality"* whilst also being shy.[111] It wasn't so much that Freddie was 'manufactured' for the stage; more that he created an authentic persona he stepped into. Freddie Mercury was a misfit in every element of his life, but he felt it was his duty to be a misfit for all the other misfits in the world. An iconic misfit. How good is that?

As Ashley Lee wrote for the LA Times in 2018:

"This is not only the persona he projected to the world, but also the person, after years of hopping continents and hiding his sexuality, he discovered in himself."[112]

Lee's article describes how Freddie channelled the mismatched parts of himself into the person he ultimately wanted to be, demonstrating that we don't have to anchor ourselves to one particular identity in order to be distinctive. For example, Freddie could honour his Zoroastrian religious roots and still be bisexual. Or he could deeply respect his family and culture, while fully embracing a new name and identity as "Freddie Mercury."

Freddie's uniqueness went beyond his persona and his artistry and extended to his physiology. Scientists who analysed his singing voice discovered he sang in a very peculiar way. Unlike most people, Freddie used his vestibular folds when he sang to create a sound known as 'subharmonics.' It's a technique used by Tuvan throat singers from Mongolia.

As Josh Jones from Open Culture said in 2017:

"Mercury's superhuman vibrato produced sounds almost no other human can make."[113]

Freddie was said to believe that his unusual teeth contributed to his incredible vocal range. More than that, they become part of his brand. As rock biographer Martin Kielty explains:

"... The image of Mercury and his prominent teeth became a trademark; so much so that actor Rami Malek had the set he used in Bohemian Rhapsody [the movie] plated in gold to be kept as a memento."[114]

Just as an iconic leader can have a signature piece of clothing or an accessory, Freddie's teeth were part of his trademark. Reading over this analysis of Freddie as an iconic brand, something that stood out to me was that all the things he was once ridiculed for became the elements of his brand that set him apart; his 'product differentiation.'

Freddie didn't care much about convention - in appearance, or music. Rejecting convention set him free to push boundaries. A good example of this is Queen's song, Bohemian Rhapsody. Unlike pop hits that played (and were remembered) for around 3 minutes, Bohemian Rhapsody was a 6-minute pop single which included an operatic passage right in the middle of the song. The production technique of overlapping sounds and musical styles was also very innovative. Queen decided that rock music and opera could, should, and would belong together.

As composer and NYU professor Irwin Fisch said in Business Insider:

"'Bohemian Rhapsody' had a very rare effect on people, which is that it was one of those songs where the first time you heard it, you hadn't heard anything like it... It's the kind of song that makes you pull over to the side of the road, because you go, 'What the devil is this?' Very few songs have done that, and that did."

Fisch continues:

"An important reason that 'Bohemian Rhapsody' resonates and has resonated for over 40 years is that it embodies something very intense, which is Freddie Mercury's personality and life. That record is an oral extension of Freddie Mercury's personality and life. That record is an oral extension of Freddie Mercury's self-consciousness without shame. It's music [in which] in some ways, the sensibilities are out of the closet. As a performer, there hadn't been a Freddie Mercury before Freddie Mercury.[115]

Freddie Mercury's music was an extension of himself.

Will there ever be another Freddie Mercury?

A true icon cannot be replicated nor manufactured, and we wouldn't want to try. We will always have Freddie Mercury and he will always be unique. But there are other icons walking around the planet right now who we're yet to discover. If you're reading this, you might be one of them!

Like Freddie, people with iconic potential go against the grain. They are the entrepreneurs flipping industries on their heads. They are the creative people mixing together ingredients we never thought to combine. They're the trailblazers and innovators who are rumbling the foundations of everything we know to be true. And they are real, vulnerable, imperfect people, facing their own unique struggles - criticism, opposition and trenchant resistance - as they rebelliously rewrite the rules.

While it's impossible to produce a standard success formula for icons like Freddie Mercury, there is one thing that remains undisputed: they are utterly dedicated to their craft. Freddie continued making music right up until he died. Even though he was dying, he told Brian May and Roger Taylor to continue writing songs for him to sing. According to the recent Bohemian Rhapsody movie, Freddie gave Queen complete creative freedom to do what they liked with his songs, on the proviso they promised to *"never make me boring."*[116] Freddie died after telling his fellow band members he needed to rest.[117]

For all the colourful parts and contrasting elements to Freddie Mercury, at the heart of it all his mission was simple. Freddie told journalist David Wigg:

"I don't have any aspirations to live to 70… As far as I'm concerned… I have lived a full life and if I'm dead tomorrow, I don't give a damn. I really have done it all, I really have."[118]

As far as Freddie was concerned, he just wanted to pack in as much life and fun as he could with the years he had left.

Freddie is forever immortalised in his music, as well as by a statue in Montreux, Switzerland, where he spent the last part of his life and recorded Queen's last album. The statue is emblazoned with the title of a solo album of Freddie's that was released in 2006:

"Lover of life, singer of songs."

It's a mission, captured in a 6-word mantra, that continues to captivate the world in unimagined ways. And perhaps that's the answer after all: throwing ourselves into life and our purpose without limits and never losing sight of our focus up until the day we die. If we were Freddie Mercury, this would mean putting our everything into each note we sang, every chord we wrote, each concert we performed, each conflicting genre of music we blended to create beautiful songs, against all odds. Sure, we'd have our sights on the big goals - maybe even iconic status - but we'd fully understand that the details in each moment mattered. I didn't know Freddie, and I can't ask him, but from what I've read it sounds like he wanted to make music above all else. But more than that, he wanted to revolutionise music.

When writing about Freddie, I recalled a profound quote that a colleague mentioned was her favourite, and it stuck with me:

"On your last day on earth, the person you became will meet the person you could have become." - Anonymous.

To me, our last day on earth is the ultimate moment of truth. Our significance is not tied to how many people approve of us or what they think of us. Rather, it's about who we became in our own eyes. It's about whether we lived our life to the full; whether we made the most of our unique talents and potential.

This has become the benchmark for how I spend my time and the products and services I create. This book is an example. Everyone might love it; some people may hate it. The critics might tear it apart or it could make the New York Times Best Seller list. No matter what happens, I put my everything into creating this for you. I felt like I was meant to write this book at this time. In fact, I felt I couldn't live without giving it to you; that something I needed to create so badly must surely be of value to others.

Whether this book is read by a million people or only one, on my last day on earth I'll be glad I wrote it. That's the true measure of its worth. If nobody buys it, it will still be valuable for taking me on this journey. But if it encourages you to accept, embrace and use your unlikeability to attain your goals and change the world, its value will increase exponentially. We are all valuable and worthy just for being who we are - and sometimes, when we step fully into ourselves, we can make magic. That's what Freddie did. So will I. So can you.

TASK: If you could create a 6-word mantra to capture your purpose in life, what would it say?

_____

_____

_____

_____

_____

'Toot Sweet' Recap:

1. Standing in your power and establishing personal boundaries can change the way people respond and interact with you.

2. We all have the right to be empowered to choose our public and private selves.

3. The very thing you or others reject about who you are could be the very clue to who you are destined to be.

FINAL WORD AND THANK YOU

With so much noise out there in the modern marketplace, we quite understandably have to be selective with how and where we invest our energy. Thank you for choosing to read this book; for entrusting me with your time and brain space. Embracing unlikeability and writing this book changed me for the better. I hope it gave you what you needed; whether that be change, healing, reassurance, love, or courage - whatever it may be.

There's a lot of learning to marinate in here. How many parts of yourself did you discover, remember, or recognise within the leaders we explored in this book: the parts you see as strengths or weaknesses, the parts you're trying to smother with a pillow, or the parts you want to fully step into? What did you learn about what motivates you or the things you fear? What did you resist? What made you leap for joy? What parts of you did you think were weaknesses, but now realise are strengths? How much of yourself did you recognise in each chapter? What did you learn about others?

How will you see the world differently now?

I'd also like to thank everyone who has contributed to my journey so far.

Thank you to my family for believing in me, especially my Dad and my husband Paul. Thank you to my kids, Stevii and Lenny, for showing me what unconditional love is. It's been beautiful watching you bloom into the amazing individuals you are. You've taught me so much. The world is your oyster.

Thank you to all the mentors throughout my life who have steered me in the right direction, who have accepted the best and worst parts of me and always seen their potential.

Thank you to all my friends who laugh at my jokes and are invaluable sounding boards.

Thank you to my clients. Without the opportunity to work with you, I wouldn't be who I am. You've changed me more than you'll ever know.

Thank you to everyone who contributed to the creation of this book. From research, to graphics, publishing, editing, media and the leaders I've written about. This is as much your gift to the world as mine. This book wouldn't have been possible without you.

Endnotes

1 Brené Brown, The Call to Courage, Netflix, 19 April 2019

2 The Babylonian Talmud: Tractate Baba Mezi'a, pp. Baba Metzia 59b, 500AD - http://www.come-and-hear.com/babamezia/babamezia_59.html

3 Anna Freud, The Ego and the Mechanisms of Defence, Karnac Books, 1992 [1936]

4 Carl Jung, Gerard Adler and RFC Hull (eds), Aion: Researches into the Phenomenology of Self, Collected Works of CG Jung, Volume 9, (Part 2), Princeton University Press, 1969 [1951]

5 Ludwig Feuerbach, Robert M Baird (ed), Stuart E Rosenbaum (ed) and George Eliot (translator), The Essence of Christianity, Prometheus Books, 1989 [1841]

6 Deepak Chopra, The Path to Love: Spiritual Strategies for Healing, Harmony, 1998 [1996]

7 Hermann Hesse, James Franco (Foreword), Damion Searls (transcriber), Demien: The Story of Emil Sinclair's Youth, Penguin Books, 2013 [1919]

8 David Eagleman, "Can we create new senses for humans?" Ted Talk, Houston, YouTube, 12 October 2010 - https://www.youtube.com/watch?v=4c1lqFXHvqI

9 David Eagleman with Jordan Harbinger, "Making Sense of the Brain," The Art of Charm (podcast), Episode 622, 1 June 2017 - Transcript available here - https://theartofcharm.com/wp-content/uploads/2018/02/Episode-622-David-Eagleman.pdf

10 Anil Seth, "Your brain hallucinates your conscious reality," Ted Talk, Ted 2017, Vancouver, BC, 26 April 2017 - https://www.ted.com/talks/anil_seth_how_your_brain_hallucinates_your_conscious_reality?language=en

11 Ichiro Kishimi and Fumitake Koga, The Courage to be Disliked, Allen & Unwin, 2017

12 Kishimi and Koga, p.49

13 Brené Brown, The Call to Courage, Netflix, 19 April 2019

14 Peggy McIntosh, "White Privilege: Unpacking the Invisible Knapsack," Peace and Freedom Magazine, Women's International League for Peace and Freedom, Philadelphia, PA, July/August 1989, pp. 10-12

15 Tracey Spicer, "Keynote Speech," Calling out financial bias and imbalance, CEDA Women in Leadership Series, West Perth, 15 June 2017 (unpublished, transcript courtesy of Tracey Spicer)

16 See, for example: Wenlei Ma, "The same resume with different names nets different results," news.com.au, 1 October 2014 - https://www.news.com.au/finance/work/careers/the-same-resume-with-different-names-nets-different-results/news-story/a2a182fb4570e948c27ce63139ee66b1

And: Rob McCormick, "Bias in Your CV: Why You May Not Be Getting Interviews," Ideal Role, 3 September 2018 - https://www.idealrole.com/blog/cv-bias

17 James St James, "These 25 Examples of Male Privilege from a Trans Guy's Perspective Really Prove the Point," Everyday Feminism, 30 May 2015 - https://everydayfeminism.com/2015/05/male-privilege-trans-men/

18 @billshortenMP, "A young Aboriginal man of 18 is more likely to end up in gaol than university. That should shock and shame us all. We've got to do better - and that starts with setting new justice targets as part of our Closing the Gap agenda," Twitter, 29 March, 2.23pm - https://twitter.com/billshortenmp/status/979212439873990656?lang=en

19 RMIT University, "Fact check: Are young Indigenous men more likely to end up in jail than university?" ABC News, 3 March 2016 - https://www.abc.net.au/news/2015-12-03/fact-check-aboriginal-men-in-jail-and-university/6907540

20 Australian Bureau of Statistics, Socio-economic Advantage and Disadvantage, 2071.0 - Census of Population and Housing: Reflecting Australia - Stories from the Census, 2016, 6 November 2018 - https://www.abs.gov.au/ausstats/abs@.nsf/Lookup/by%20Subject/2071.0~2016~Main%20Features~Socio-Economic%20Advantage%20and%20Disadvantage~123

21 Creative Bloq Staff (Computer Arts), "20 milestones in the history of branding," Creative Bloq, 18 September 2015 - https://www.creativebloq.com/branding/milestones-history-branding-91516855

22 Timothy Ingram, "How branding has changed," Medium, 13 June 2016 - https://medium.com/@timothyingram/how-branding-has-changed-5e9706f5b259

23 Ron Malhotra, "The Power of Intrigue," LinkedIn, June 2019 - https://www.linkedin.com/posts/ronmalhotra_ronmalhotra-marketing-magnify-activity-6546367541927911425-KhGr

24 Rohit Bhargava, Likenomics: The Unexpected Truth Behind Earning Trust, Influencing Behaviour, and Inspiring Action, John Wiley & Sons, 2012

25 Danny Schechter, "Nelson Mandela's contested legacy," Al Jazeera, 16 July 2011 - https://www.aljazeera.com/indepth/opinion/2011/07/201172141053378510.html

26 John Carlin in Rohit Bhargava, "Introduction: Likeability, Rogue Economics, and the Lovable Fool," in Likenomics: The Unexpected Truth Behind Earning Trust, Influencing Behaviour, and Inspiring Action, John Wiley & Sons, 2012

27 Mark Gevisser, "Mandela's failures as well as successes must be recognized," The New Daily, 8 December 2013 - https://thenewdaily.com.au/news/world/2013/12/08/mandelas-successes-failures-must-recognised/

28 Matthew Stadlen, "Maki Mandela: 'I'm very proud of my father - but he was not perfect or a saint," The Telegraph, UK, 14 October 2015 - https://www.telegraph.co.uk/news/worldnews/nelson-mandela/11931955/Maki-Mandela-Im-very-proud-of-my-father-but-he-was-not-perfect-or-a-saint.html

29 Olivia Waxman, "The U.S. had Nelson Mandela on Terrorist Watch Lists Until 2008. Here's Why," TIME, 18 July 2018 - https://time.com/5338569/nelson-mandela-terror-list/

30 Robyn Dixon, "Nelson Mandela's legacy: As a leader, he was willing to use violence," Los Angeles Times, 6 December 2013 - https://www.latimes.com/world/worldnow/la-fg-wn-nelson-mandela-legacy-violence-20131206-story.html

31 Fred Bridgland, "Nelson Mandela: A twentieth century hero," The Scotsman, 7 December 2013 - https://www.scotsman.com/news/politics/nelson-mandela-a-twentieth-century-hero-1-3224049

32 Alan Hirsch, "How compromises and mistakes made in the Mandela era hobbled South Africa's economy," The Conversation, 23 December 2015 - https://theconversation.com/how-compromises-and-mistakes-made-in-the-mandela-era-hobbled-south-africas-economy-52156

33 See, for example: Rhonda Reaves, "Retaliatory Harassment: Sex and the Hostile Coworker as the Enforcer of Workplace Norms," Florida A&M University College of Law, Summer 2007, p. 409 - https://commons.law.famu.edu/cgi/viewcontent.cgi?referer=https://www.google.com/&httpsredir=1&article=1046&context=faculty-research

34 Dr Pragya Agarwal, "Not Very Likeable: Here Is How Bias Is Affecting Women Leaders," Forbes, 23 October 2018 - https://www.forbes.com/sites/pragyaagarwaleurope/2018/10/23/not-very-likeable-here-is-how-bias-is-affecting-women-leaders/#35af17e295fd

35 Corinne A Moss-Racusin et al, "When Men Break the Gender Rules: Status Incongruity and Backlash Against Modest Men," Psychology of Men & Maculinity, Vol. 11, No. 2, April 2010, pp. 140-151 - https://www.researchgate.net/publication/232464622_When_Men_Break_the_Gender_Rules_Status_Incongruity_and_Backlash_Against_Modest_Men

36 Ashleigh Shelby Rosette et al, "Are male leaders penalized for seeking help?" The Leadership Quarterly, 26, 2015, pp. 749–762 - https://klm68f.media.zestyio.com/shelby-rosette_mueller_lebel_2015-lq-leadership-and-asking-for-help.pdf

37 See, for example: Julie E Phelan et al, "Competent Yet Out in the Cold: Shifting Criteria for Hiring Reflect Backlash Toward Agentic Women," Psychology of Women Quarterly, Vol. 32, Issue 4, 2008 - https://journals.sagepub.com/doi/abs/10.1111/j.1471-6402.2008.00454.x?journalCode=pwqa

38 Jeanine L Prime et al, "Women 'Take Care,' Men 'Take Charge': Managers' Stereotypic Perceptions of Women and Men Leaders," Psychologist-Manager Journal, Vol. 11, No. 2, August 2008, pp. 1-44 - http://cbafiles.unl.edu/public/cbainternal/facStaffUploads/women%20take%20care.2009.published.pdf

39 Kristen Bellstrom, "Female CEOs Are More Likely to Be Fired Than Men—Even When Their Companies Are Thriving," Fortune, 30 November 2018 - https://fortune.com/2018/11/30/female-ceo-fired-study/

40 Clara Kulich and Michelle K Ryan, "The Glass Cliff," January 2017 - https://www.researchgate.net/publication/310799724_The_glass_cliff

41 Vishal K Gupta et al, "You're Fired! Gender Disparities in CEO Dismissal," Journal of Management, 5 November 2018 - https://journals.sagepub.com/doi/abs/10.1177/0149206318810415#articleCitationDownloadContainer

42 Emily Peck, "When Company Is Failing, Female CEOs Get Blamed More Frequently Than Men," Huffington Post, 26 October 2016 - https://www.huffingtonpost.com.au/entry/female-ceo-blame_n_58100af0e4b001e247df34c5

43 David M Mayer, "How Men Get Penalized for Straying from Masculine Norms," Harvard Business Review, 8 October 2018 - https://hbr.org/2018/10/how-men-get-penalized-for-straying-from-masculine-norms

44 Elizabeth Semmelhack in William Kremer, "Why did men stop wearing high heels?," BBC News, 25 January 2013 - https://www.bbc.com/news/magazine-21151350

45 Amanda Montell, "From 4000 BCE To Today: The Fascinating History of Men and Makeup," Byrdie, 7 March 2019 - https://www.byrdie.com/history-makeup-gender

46 Tariq Zaidi, "There's no Tinder in the desert: How Chad's Wodaabe nomads find love," Adventure.com, 27 August 2018 - https://adventure.com/wodaabe-nomads-gerewol-chad-africa/

47 Ladies' Home Journal 1918 in Margaret Hartmann, "The History Of Pink For Girls, Blue For Boys," Jezebel, 10 April 2011 - https://jezebel.com/the-history-of-pink-for-girls-blue-for-boys-5790638

48 David P Schmitt, "The Truth About Sex Differences," Psychology Today, 7 November 2017 - https://www.psychologytoday.com/intl/articles/201711/the-truth-about-sex-differences

49 @jvn (Jonathan Van Ness), Twitter, 26 August 2019 - https://twitter.com/jvn/status/1166168929103962117

50 Ella Chochrek, "Celebrating Gender Non-Conformist Style in Bold Looks at the VMAs", Footwear News (FN), 26 August 2019 - https://footwearnews.com/2019/fashion/celebrity-style/gender-non-binary-outfit-trend-mtv-vmas-2019-1202822431/

51 Brenda L Russell and Debra Oswald, "When Sexism Cuts Both Ways: Predictors of Tolerance of Sexual Harassment of Men," Men and Masculinities, Vol. 19, Issue 5, 2015 - https://journals.sagepub.com/doi/full/10.1177/1097184X15602745

52 Anne Summers, "Bill Shorten's biggest challenge is to make himself more likeable," The Sydney Morning Herald, 8 September 2017 - https://www.smh.com.au/opinion/bill-shortens-biggest-challenge-is-to-make-himself-more-likeable-20170908-gydbcl.html

53 David Marr, "Faction Man: Bill Shorten's Path to Power," Quarterly Essay, No. 59, September 2015 - https://www.quarterlyessay.com.au/essay/2015/09/faction-man/extract

54 David Knights and Maria Tullberg, "Managing masculinity/mismanaging the corporation," Organization 19(4), 2012, pp. 385-404

55 Laurie A Rudman et al, "Reactions to gender egalitarian men: Perceived feminization due to stigma-by-association," Group Processes & Intergroup Relations, Vol.16, Issue 5, 2013, pp. 572–599 - https://journals.sagepub.com/doi/abs/10.1177/1368430212461160#articleCitationDownloadContainer

56 Ichiro Kishimi and Fumitake Koga, The Courage to be Disliked, Allen & Unwin, 2017

57 Jordan Daykin, "The Art and Science in Business," Forbes, 19 December 2018 - https://www.forbes.com/sites/jordandaykin/2018/12/19/the-art-and-science-in-business/#76df75a5a7c5

58 Shirley Halperin, "Amy Winehouse Remembered: A Unique Artist Gone Too Soon, But Not Forgotten," Hollywood Reporter, 23 July 2011 - https://www.hollywoodreporter.com/news/amy-winehouse-remembered-a-unique-214672

59 Mark Cooper, "The unique legacy of Amy Winehouse at the BBC," BBC, 21 June 2015 - https://www.bbc.co.uk/music/articles/4700eb2a-01d3-4559-902f-e9753602fd37

60 Nick Shymansky in Kathryn Bromwich, "Amy Winehouse's manager Nick Shymansky: 'She'd be so sweet and funny, but there were warning signs…,'" The Guardian, 14 June 2015 - https://www.theguardian.com/music/2015/jun/14/amy-winehouse-manager-nick-shymansky-interview

61 Elena Cleaves, "8 Aspects of Amy Winehouse's Legacy More Important Than Her Addiction," Elite Daily, 8 July 2015 - https://www.elitedaily.com/entertainment/film/components-winehouse-legacy/1102295

62 Amy Winehouse in "Amy Winehouse Unpublished Interview From 2004 - 'I Never Want To Remember Anything Bad In My Life,'" The Huffington Post, UK, 18 July 2014 - https://www.huffingtonpost.co.uk/2014/07/18/amy-winehouse-unpublished-interview-2004_n_5598705.html

63 Leena Tailor, "Fall Preview 2018: How Lady Gaga Conquered Music, Fashion and Film in Just a Decade," ET Online, 4 September 2018 - https://www.etonline.com/how-lady-gaga-conquered-music-fashion-and-film-fall-preview-106993

64 Lady Gaga in Julie Gerstein, "11 Things We Learned From Lady Gaga's Google Moderator Interview," Vulture, 23 March 2011 - https://www.vulture.com/2011/03/11_things_we_learned_from_lad

65 Lady Gaga, "When I was young …," Instagram, 10 July 2019 - https://www.instagram.com/p/BztP4qeFFiw/?utm_source=ig_embed

66 Jane Fynes-Clinton, "Lady Gaga's grab for attention enough to make you gag," The Courier Mail, 15 September 2010 - https://www.couriermail.com.au/news/lady-gagas-grab-for-attention-enough-to-make-you-gag/story-e6freri6-1225923966643?sv=b2898a7907e420830b9d519b7f6c88ea

67 Camille Paglia, "Lady Gaga and the death of sex," The Times, 12 September 2010 - https://www.thetimes.co.uk/article/lady-gaga-and-the-death-of-sex-lnzbcd70zj3

68 Lady Gaga and Jeppe Laursen, "Born This Way," Born This Way, Interscope Records, 23 May 2011

69 Jacob Seferian, "Unpopular Opinion: Lady Gaga Shouldn't Win The Oscar," Wussy, 23 January 2019 - https://www.wussymag.com/all/2019/1/23/unpopular-opinion-lady-gaga-shouldnt-win-the-oscar

70 Lauren Duca, "Lady Gaga Was The Biggest Pop Star In The World. What Happened?" The Huffington Post, 12 July 2017 - https://www.huffingtonpost.com.au/2015/02/18/middlebrow-lady-gaga_n_6708638.html

71 Helen Holmes, "Revisiting Lady Gaga's 'Artpop' Five Years Later," Observer, 6 November 2018 - https://observer.com/2018/11/revisiting-lady-gagas-artpop-five-years-later/

72 Baba Shiv in Eilene Zimmerman, "Baba Shiv: Failure is the Mother of Innovation," Insights by Stanford Business, 2 March 2016 - https://www.gsb.stanford.edu/insights/baba-shiv-failure-mother-innovation

73 Lucy Stone, "The meeting that drove Netflix founders to bankrupt Blockbuster," Brisbane TImes, 8 July 2019 - https://www.brisbanetimes.com.au/national/queensland/the-meeting-that-drove-netflix-s-founders-to-bankrupt-blockbuster-20190708-p5255f.html

74 Lindsay Zoladz, "Lady Gaga goes to the middle," Vulture, New York Magazine, 13 July 2015 - https://www.vulture.com/2015/07/lady-gaga-goes-normal.htm

75 Lady Gaga in Chris Moukarbel (director), Gaga: Five Foot Two, Netflix, 22 September 2017

76 Lady Gaga, "When I was young …", Instagram, 10 July 2019 - https://www.instagram.com/p/BztP4qeFFiw/?utm_source=ig_embed

77 Wiebke Bleidorn, Christopher Hopwood and Richard E Lucas, "Life events and Personality Trait Change," Journal of Personality, 86(1), February 2018, pp. 83-96 - https://www.ncbi.nlm.nih.gov/pubmed/27716921

78 Mathias Allemand and Christoph Flückiger, "Changing Personality Traits: Some Considerations From Psychotherapy Process -Outcome Research for Intervention Efforts on Intentional Personality Change," Journal of Psychotherapy Integration, 27(4), June 2017 - https://www.zoraprod.uzh.ch/id/eprint/145592/1/Allemand_&_Fluckiger_final.pdf

79 Allemand and Flückiger

80 BP Chapman, S Hampson and J Clarkin, 2014 in Allemand and Flückiger

81 @hauslabs (Haus Laboratories), "Our tools were designed with artistry …," Instagram, 10 July 2019 - https://www.instagram.com/p/BztInPLltnP/?hl=en

82 @hauslabs (Haus Laboratories), "ONE MORE DAY. There are NO RULES …," Instagram, 10 July 2019 - https://www.instagram.com/p/Bz5vn0fFxiU/?hl=en

83 Lady Gaga with Marissa Mayer, "Lady Gaga: 'Google Goes Gaga,'" Musicians at Google, YouTube, 22 March 2011, at 0:38:15 - http://www.youtube.com/watch?v=hNa_-1d_0tA&t=38m15s

84 Lady Gaga with Marissa Mayer, at 0:14:42 - http://www.youtube.com/watch?v=hNa_-1d_0tA&t=14m42s

85 Yassmin Abdel-Magied with Yana Fry, "Finding Yourself Despite Being Different," Yana TV, YouTube and Connected Women, 9 September 2016, at 0:5:38 - https://www.connectedwomen.co/magazine/how-yassmin-abdel-magied-found-herself-despite-being-different-video/

86 Yassmin Abdel-Magied, "I Tried to Fight Racism by Being a 'Model Minority' - and Then It Backfired," Teen Vogue, 28 September 2017 - https://www.teenvogue.com/story/fight-racism-model-minority-yassmin-abdel-magied

87 Yassmin Abdel-Magied, Teen Vogue

88 Jon Ronson, So You've Been Publicly Shamed, Picador, 2015

89 Helen Lewis, "The digital ducking stool," New Statesman America, 11 March 2015 - https://www.newstatesman.com/culture/2015/03/digital-ducking-stool

90 Kate Ashton, "Adam Goodes 'cut down' by racist booing because he was powerful, says commentator Charlie King", ABC, 22 July 2019 - https://www.abc.net.au/news/2019-07-21/adam-goodes-faced-racism-because-he-was-powerful-charlie-king/11328552

91 Michael Safi, "AFL great Adam Goodes is being booed across Australia. How did it come to this?", The Guardian, 29 July 2015 - https://www.theguardian.com/sport/blog/2015/jul/29/afl-great-adam-goodes-is-being-booed-across-australia-how-did-it-come-to-this

92 Adam Goodes, "Adam Goodes' response to the racism incident against Collingwood R9 2013," Swans TV, YouTube, 27 May 2013, at 0:1:10 - http://www.youtube.com/watch?v=iZkquBdLm0E&t=1m10s

93 Stephen Rodrick, "Serena Williams: The Great One," Rolling Stone, 18 June 2013 - https://www.rollingstone.com/culture/culture-sports/serena-williams-the-great-one-88694/

94 Ben Rothenberg, "Tennis's Top Women Balance Body Image with Ambition," The New York Times, 10 July 2015 - https://www.nytimes.com/2015/07/11/sports/tennis/tenniss-top-women-balance-body-image-with-quest-for-success.html?smid=tw-nytimes&_r=2&referrer=

95 Ben Rothenberg

96 Stephen Rodrick, "Serena Williams: The Great One," Rolling Stone, 18 June 2013 - https://www.rollingstone.com/culture/culture-sports/serena-williams-the-great-one-88694/

97 Stephen Rodrick

98 ESPN News Services, "Naomi Osaka wins controversial 2018 US Open; Serena Williams fined, penalized game for calling chair umpire 'a thief,'" 10 September 2018 - https://www.espn.com.au/tennis/story/_/id/24617080/naomi-osaka-wins-controversial-2018-us-open-serena-williams

99 Jerry Bembry, "Serena Williams deserves share of blame for her actions," The Undefeated, 10 September 2018 - https://theundefeated.com/features/serena-williams-deserves-share-of-blame-for-her-actions/

100 Jerry Bembry

101 Elizabeth Kiefer, "Serena Williams And The Double Blind Of Emotional Women," Girlboss, 14 September 2018 - https://www.girlboss.com/identity/serena-williams-naomi-osaka-us-open

102 George Orwell, Don Watson (Introduction), Animal Farm, Text Publishing, 2014

103 Associated Press, "Serena Williams accuses umpire of sexism and vows to 'fight for women,'" The Guardian, 9 September 2018 - https://www.theguardian.com/sport/2018/sep/09/serena-williams-accuses-officials-of-sexism-and-vows-to-fight-for-women

104 Yasmin Noon, "The Life of a Chef", Australian Ageing Agenda, 3 July 2013 - https://www.australianageingagenda.com.au/2013/07/03/profile-the-life-of-a-chef/

105 Spencer, Charles, 9th Earl Spencer, "Earl Spencer's Funeral Oration," BBC, 6 September 1997 - http://www.bbc.co.uk/news/special/politics97/diana/spencerfull.html

106 Hilary Mantel, "The princess myth: Hilary Mantel on Diana," The Guardian, 26 August 2017 - https://www.theguardian.com/books/2017/aug/26/the-princess-myth-hilary-mantel-on-diana

107 Maureen Callahan, "The truth about Princess Diana and the myth she created," New York Post, 26 June 2017 - https://nypost.com/2017/06/26/how-diana-carefully-crafted-her-image-as-the-peoples-princess/

108 Taylor Swift, Max Martin and Shellback, Shake It Off, 1989, Big Machine Records, 2014

109 Charles Dickens, Great Expectations, Courier Corporation, 2012 [1881], p. 55

110 Roger Taylor (and Brian May) with Mike Morris and Kathryn Holloway (interviewers), "Roger Taylor and Brian May Interview One Week After Freddie Mercury Death," TV-AM, ITV, December 1991, published on YouTube, 13 February 2019 - https://www.youtube.com/watch?v=XC2RfXMkrT0

111 Roger Taylor (and Brian May) with Mike Morris and Kathryn Holloway (interviewers), "Roger Taylor and Brian May Interview One Week After Freddie Mercury Death," TV-AM, ITV, December 1991, published on YouTube, 13 February 2019 - https://www.youtube.com/watch?v=XC2RfXMkrT0

112 Ashley Lee, "'Bohemian Rhapsody' glosses over Freddy Mercury's roots and religion - just like he did," Los Angeles Times, 2 November 2018 - https://www.latimes.com/entertainment/movies/la-et-mn-freddie-mercury-race-religion-name-change-20181102-story.html

113 Josh Jones, "What Made Freddie Mercury the Greatest Vocalist in Rock History? The Secrets Revealed in a Short Video Essay," Open Culture, 20 November 2017 -http://www.openculture.com/2017/11/what-made-freddie-mercury-the-greatest-vocalist-in-rock-history-the-secrets-revealed-in-a-short-video-essay.htm

114 Martin Kielty, "How Come Freddie Mercury Never Fixed His Teeth?" UCR (Ultimate Classic Rock), 28 October 2018 - https://ultimateclassicrock.com/freddie-mercury-teeth/

115 Irwin Fisch in Nathaniel Lee, "Bohemian Rhapsody: The 6-minute rock single that changed the face of music," Business Insider Australia, 9 November 2018 - https://www.businessinsider.com.au/bohemian-rhapsody-queen-greatest-song-written-freddie-mercury-2018-10?r=US&IR=T

116 Kate Stables, "Bohemian Rhapsody review: Freddie Mercury, tied up with a bow," BFI, UK, 26 February 2019 - https://www.bfi.org.uk/news-opinion/sight-sound-magazine/reviews-recommendations/bohemian-rhapsody-freddie-mercury-queen-biopic-trite-tidy

117 Eurasia Diary, "The Freddie Mercury You Didn't Know - Life, Love and Music," ED News, 12 November 2018 - https://ednews.net/en/news/culture/335288-the-freddie-mercury-you-didnt-know

118 Freddie Mercury with David Wigg, "Ibiza 1987, part 2 - Montserrat Cabal," transcript, The David Wigg Interviews, Ultimate Queen, 1987 - http://www.ultimatequeen.co.uk/freddie-mercury/miscellaneous/david-wigg-interviews.htm#Ibiza%201987%20-%20part%202%20-%20Montserrat%20Caballe

Bibliography

@billshortenMP, "A young Aboriginal man of 18 is more likely to end up in gaol than university. That should shock and shame us all. We've got to do better - and that starts with setting new justice targets as part of our Closing the Gap agenda," Twitter, 29 March, 2.23pm - https://twitter.com/billshortenmp/status/979212439873990656?lang=en

@hauslabs (Haus Laboratories), "Our tools were designed with artistry ...," Instagram, 10 July 2019 - https://www.instagram.com/p/BztInPLltnP/?hl=en

Abdel-Magied, Yassmin, "I Tried to Fight Racism by Being a 'Model Minority' - and Then It Backfired," Teen Vogue, 28 September 2017 - https://www.teenvogue.com/story/fight-racism-model-minority-yassmin-abdel-magied

Abdel-Magied, Yassmin with Yana Fry, "Finding Yourself Despite Being Different," Yana TV, YouTube and Connected Women, 9 September 2016, at 5:38 - https://www.connectedwomen.co/magazine/how-yassmin-abdel-magied-found-herself-despite-being-different-video/

Agarwal, Pragya, "Not Very Likeable: Here Is How Bias Is Affecting Women Leaders," Forbes, 23 October 2018 - https://www.forbes.com/sites/pragyaagarwaleurope/2018/10/23/not-very-likeable-here-is-how-bias-is-affecting-women-leaders/#35af17e295fd

Allemand, Mathias and Christoph Flückiger, "Changing Personality Traits: Some Considerations From Psychotherapy Process - Outcome Research for Intervention Efforts on Intentional Personality Change", Journal of Psychotherapy Integration, 27(4), June 2017 - https://www.zoraprod.uzh.ch/id/eprint/145592/1/Allemand_&_Fluckiger_final.pdf

Ashton, Kate, "Adam Goodes 'cut down' by racist booing because he was powerful, says commentator Charlie King," ABC, 22 July 2019 - https://www.abc.net.au/news/2019-07-21/adam-goodes-faced-racism-because-he-was-powerful-charlie-king/11328552

Associated Press, "Serena Williams accuses umpire of sexism and vows to 'fight for women,'" The Guardian, 9 September 2018 - https://www.theguardian.com/sport/2018/sep/09/serena-williams-accuses-officials-of-sexism-and-vows-to-fight-for-women

Australian Bureau of Statistics, Socio-economic Advantage and Disadvantage, 2071.0 - Census of Population and Housing: Reflecting Australia - Stories from the Census, 2016, 6 November 2018 - https://www.abs.gov.au/ausstats/abs@.nsf/Lookup/by%20Subject/2071.0~2016~Main%20Features~Socio-Economic%20Advantage%20and%20Disadvantage~123

Bellstrom, Kristen, "Female CEOs Are More Likely to Be Fired Than Men—Even When Their Companies Are Thriving," Fortune, 30 November 2018 - https://fortune.com/2018/11/30/female-ceo-fired-study/

Bembry, Jerry, "Serena Williams deserves share of blame for her actions," The Undefeated, 10 September 2018 - https://theundefeated.com/features/serena-williams-deserves-share-of-blame-for-her-actions/

Bhargava, Rohit, Likenomics: The Unexpected Truth Behind Earning Trust, Influencing Behaviour, and Inspiring Action, John Wiley & Sons, 2012

Bleidorn, Wiebke, Christopher Hopwood and Richard E Lucas, "Life events and Personality Trait Change," Journal of Personality, 86(1), February 2018, pp. 83-96 - https://www.ncbi.nlm.nih.gov/pubmed/27716921

Bridgland, Fred, "Nelson Mandela: A twentieth century hero," The Scotsman, 7 December 2013 - https://www.scotsman.com/news/politics/nelson-mandela-a-twentieth-century-hero-1-3224049

Brown, Brené, The Call to Courage, Netflix, 19 April 2019

Callahan, Maureen, "The truth about Princess Diana and the myth she created," New York Post, 26 June 2017 - https://nypost.com/2017/06/26/how-diana-carefully-crafted-her-image-as-the-peoples-princess/

Carlin, John in Rohit Bhargava, "Introduction: Likeability, Rogue Economics, and the Lovable Fool" in Likenomics: The Unexpected Truth Behind Earning Trust, Influencing Behaviour, and Inspiring Action, John Wiley & Sons, 2012

Chapman, B P, S Hampson and J Clarkin, "Personality-informed interventions for healthy aging: Conclusions from a National Institute on Aging Work Group," Developmental Psychology, 50, 2014, pp. 1426-144, quoted in Mathias Allemand and Christoph Flückiger, "Changing Personality Traits: Some Considerations From Psychotherapy Process -Outcome Research for Intervention Efforts on Intentional Personality Change," Journal of Psychotherapy Integration, 27(4), June 2017 - https://www.zoraprod.uzh.ch/id/eprint/145592/1/Allemand_&_Fluckiger_final.pdf

Chochrek, Ella, "Celebrating Gender Non-Conformist Style in Bold Looks at the VMAs," Footwear News (FN), 26 August 2019 - https://footwearnews.com/2019/fashion/celebrity-style/gender-non-binary-outfit-trend-mtv-vmas-2019-1202822431/

Chopra, Deepak, The Path to Love: Spiritual Strategies for Healing, Harmony, 1998 [1996]

Cleaves, Elena, "8 Aspects of Amy Winehouse's Legacy More Important Than Her Addiction," Elite Daily, 8 July 2015 - https://www.elitedaily.com/entertainment/film/components-winehouse-legacy/1102295

Cooper, Mark, "The unique legacy of Amy Winehouse at the BBC," BBC, 21 June 2015 - https://www.bbc.co.uk/music/articles/4700eb2a-01d3-4559-902f-e9753602fd37

Creative Bloq Staff (Computer Arts), "20 milestones in the history of branding," Creative Bloq, 18 September 2015 - https://www.creativebloq.com/branding/milestones-history-branding-91516855

Daykin, Jordan, "The Art and Science in Business," Forbes, 19 December 2018 - https://www.forbes.com/sites/jordandaykin/2018/12/19/the-art-and-science-in-business/#76df75a5a7c5

Dickens, Charles, Great Expectations, Courier Corporation, 2012 [1881], p. 55

Dixon, Robyn Dixon, "Nelson Mandela's legacy: As a leader, he was willing to use violence," Los Angeles Times, 6 December 2013 - https://www.latimes.com/world/worldnow/la-fg-wn-nelson-mandela-legacy-violence-20131206-story.html

Duca, Lauren, "Lady Gaga Was The Biggest Pop Star In The World. What Happened?" The Huffington Post, 12 July 2017 - https://www.huffingtonpost.com.au/2015/02/18/middlebrow-lady-gaga_n_6708638.html

Eagleman, David, "Can we create new senses for humans?" Ted Talk, Houston, YouTube, 12 October 2010 - https://www.youtube.com/watch?v=4c1lqFXHvqI

Eagleman, David with Jordan Harbinger, "Making Sense of the Brain," The Art of Charm (podcast), Episode 622, 1 June 2017 - Transcript available here - https://theartofcharm-theartofcharminc.netdna-ssl.com/wp-content/uploads/2018/02/Episode-622-David-Eagleman.pdf

ESPN News Services, "Naomi Osaka wins controversial 2018 US Open; Serena Williams fined, penalized game for calling chair umpire 'a thief,'" 10 September 2018 - https://www.espn.com.au/tennis/story/_/id/24617080/naomi-osaka-wins-controversial-2018-us-open-serena-williams

Eurasia Diary, "The Freddie Mercury You Didn't Know - Life, Love and Music," ED News, 12 November 2018 - https://ednews.net/en/news/culture/335288-the-freddie-mercury-you-didnt-know

Feuerbach, Ludwig, Robert M Baird (ed.), Stuart E Rosenbaum (ed.) and George Eliot (translator), The Essence of Christianity, Prometheus Books, 1989

Fisch, Irwin in Nathaniel Lee, "Bohemian Rhapsody: The 6-minute rock single that changed the face of music," Business Insider Australia, 9 November 2018 - https://www.businessinsider.com.au/bohemian-rhapsody-queen-greatest-song-written-freddie-mercury-2018-10?r=US&IR=T

Freud, Anna, The Ego and the Mechanisms of Defence, Karnac Books, 1992 [1936]

Jane Fynes-Clinton, "Lady Gaga's grab for attention enough to make you gag," The Courier Mail, 15 September 2010 - https://www.couriermail.com.au/news/lady-gagas-grab-for-attention-enough-to-make-you-gag/story-e6freri6-1225923966643?sv=b2898a7907e420830b9d519b7f6c88ea

Gevisser, Mark, "Mandela's failures as well as successes must be recognized," The New Daily, 8 December 2013 - https://thenewdaily.com.au/news/world/2013/12/08/mandelas-successes-failures-must-recognised/

Goodes, Adam, "Adam Goodes' response to the racism incident against Collingwood R9 2013," Swans TV, YouTube, 27 May 2013, at 0:1:10 - http://www.youtube.com/watch?v=iZkquBdLm0E&t=1m10s

Gupta, Vishal K, Sandra C Mortal, Sabatino Silveri, Minxing Sun and Daniel B Turban, "You're Fired! Gender Disparities in CEO Dismissal," Journal of Management, 5 November 2018 - https://journals.sagepub.com/doi/abs/10.1177/0149206318810415#articleCitationDownloadContainer

Halperin, Shirley, "Amy Winehouse Remembered: A Unique Artist Gone Too Soon, But Not Forgotten," Hollywood Reporter, 23 July 2011 - https://www.hollywoodreporter.com/news/amy-winehouse-remembered-a-unique-214672

Hesse, Hermann, James Franco (Foreword), Damion Searls (Transcriber), Demien: The Story of Emil Sinclair's Youth, Penguin Books, 2013 [1919]

Hirsch, Alan, "How compromises and mistakes made in the Mandela era hobbled South Africa's economy," The Conversation, 23 December 2015 - https://theconversation.com/how-compromises-and-mistakes-made-in-the-mandela-era-hobbled-south-africas-economy-52168

Holmes, Helen, "Revisiting Lady Gaga's 'Artpop' Five Years Later," Observer, 6 November 2018 - https://observer.com/2018/11/revisiting-lady-gagas-artpop-five-years-later/

Ingram, Timothy, "How branding has changed," Medium, 13 June 2016 - https://medium.com/@timothyingram/how-branding-has-changed-5e9706f5b259

Jones, Josh, "What Made Freddie Mercury the Greatest Vocalist in Rock History? The Secrets Revealed in a Short Video Essay," Open Culture, 20 November 2017 - http://www.openculture.com/2017/11/what-made-freddie-mercury-the-greatest-vocalist-in-rock-history-the-secrets-revealed-in-a-short-video-essay.html

Jung, Carl, Aion: Researches into the Phenomenology of Self, Collected Works of CG Jung, Volume 9, (Part 2), Gerard Adler and RFC Hull (eds), Princeton University Press, 1969

Kiefer, Elizabeth, "Serena Williams And The Double Blind Of Emotional Women," Girlboss, 14 September 2018 - https://www.girlboss.com/identity/serena-williams-naomi-osaka-us-open

Kielty, Martin, "How Come Freddie Mercury Never Fixed His Teeth?" UCR (Ultimate Classic Rock), 28 October 2018 - https://ultimateclassicrock.com/freddie-mercury-teeth/

Kishimi, Ichiro and Fumitake Koga, The Courage to be Disliked, Allen & Unwin, 2017

Knights, David and Maria Tullberg, "Managing masculinity/mismanaging the corporation," Organization 19(4), 2012, pp. 385-404

Kulich, Clara and Michelle K Ryan, "The Glass Cliff," January 2017 - https://www.researchgate.net/publication/310799724_The_glass_cliff

Ladies' Home Journal 1918 in Margaret Hartmann, "The History Of Pink For Girls, Blue For Boys", Jezebel, 10 April 2011 - https://jezebel.com/the-history-of-pink-for-girls-blue-for-boys-5790638

Lady Gaga, "When I was young …," Instagram, 10 July 2019 - https://www.instagram.com/p/BztP4qeFFiw/?utm_source=ig_embed

Lady Gaga and Jeppe Laursen, "Born This Way", Born This Way, Interscope Records, 23 May 2011

Lady Gaga in Julie Gerstein, "11 Things We Learned From Lady Gaga's Google Moderator Interview," Vulture, 23 March 2011 - https://www.vulture.com/2011/03/11_things_we_learned_from_lad

Lady Gaga in Chris Moukarbel (director), Gaga: Five Foot Two, Netflix, 22 September 2017

Lady Gaga with Marissa Mayer, "Lady Gaga: 'Google Goes Gaga,'" Musicians at Google, YouTube, 22 March 2011, at 0:38:15 and 0:14:42 - http://www.youtube.com/watch?v=hNa_-1d_0tA&t=38m15s - http://www.youtube.com/watch?v=hNa_-1d_0tA&t=14m42s

Lee, Ashley, "'Bohemian Rhapsody' glosses over Freddy Mercury's roots and religion - just like he did," Los Angeles Times, 2 November 2018 - https://www.latimes.com/entertainment/movies/la-et-mn-freddie-mercury-race-religion-name-change-20181102-story.html

Lewis, Helen, "The digital ducking stool," New Statesman America, 11 March 2015 - https://www.newstatesman.com/culture/2015/03/digital-ducking-stool

Ma, Wenlei, "The same resume with different names nets different results," news.com.au, 1 October 2014 - https://www.news.com.au/finance/work/careers/the-same-resume-with-different-names-nets-different-results/news-story/a2a182fb4570e948c27ce63139ee66b1

Ron Malhotra, "The Power of Intrigue," LinkedIn, June 2019 - https://www.linkedin.com/posts/ronmalhotra_ronmalhotra-marketing-magnify-activity-6546367541927911425-KhGr

Mantel, Hilary, "The princess myth: Hilary Mantel on Diana," The Guardian, 26 August 2017 - https://www.theguardian.com/books/2017/aug/26/the-princess-myth-hilary-mantel-on-diana

Marr, David, "Faction Man: Bill Shorten's Path to Power," Quarterly Essay, No. 59, September 2015 - https://www.quarterlyessay.com.au/essay/2015/09/faction-man/extract

Mayer, David M, "How Men Get Penalized for Straying from Masculine Norms," Harvard Business Review, 8 October 2018 - https://hbr.org/2018/10/how-men-get-penalized-for-straying-from-masculine-norms

Moss-Racusin, Corinne A, Julie E Phelan and Laurie Rudman, "When Men Break the Gender Rules: Status Incongruity and Backlash Against Modest Men," Psychology of Men & Maculinity, Vol. 11, No. 2, April 2010, pp. 140-151 - https://www.researchgate.net/publication/232464622_When_Men_Break_the_Gender_Rules_Status_Incongruity_and_Backlash_Against_Modest_Men

Noon, Yasmin, "The life of a Chef," Australian Ageing Agenda, 3 July 2013 - https://www.australianageingagenda.com.au/2013/07/03/profile-the-life-of-a-chef/

McCormick, Rob, "Bias in Your CV: Why You May Not Be Getting Interviews," Ideal Role, 3 September 2018 - https://www.idealrole.com/blog/cv-bias

McIntosh, Peggy, "White Privilege: Unpacking the Invisible Knapsack," Peace and Freedom Magazine, Women's International League for Peace and Freedom, Philadelphia, PA, July/August 1989, pp. 10-12

Mercury, Freddie with David Wigg, "Ibiza 1987, part 2 - Montserrat Cabal," transcript, The David Wigg Interviews, Ultimate Queen, 1987 - http://www.ultimatequeen.co.uk/freddie-mercury/miscellaneous/david-wigg-interviews.htm#Ibiza%201987%20-%20part%202%20-%20Montserrat%20Caballe

Montell, Amanda, "From 4000 BCE To Today: The Fascinating History of Men and Makeup," Byrdie, 7 March 2019 - https://www.byrdie.com/history-makeup-gender

Orwell, George, Don Watson (Introduction), Animal Farm, Text Publishing, 2014

Paglia, Camille, "Lady Gaga and the death of sex," The Times, 12 September 2010 - https://www.thetimes.co.uk/article/lady-gaga-and-the-death-of-sex-lnzbcd70zj3

Peck, Emily, "When Company Is Failing, Female CEOs Get Blamed More Frequently Than Men", Huffington Post, 26 October 2016 - https://www.huffingtonpost.com.au/entry/female-ceo-blame_n_58100af0e4b001e247df34c5

Phelan, Julie E, Corinne A Moss-Racusin and Laurie A Rudman, "Competent Yet Out in the Cold: Shifting Criteria for Hiring Reflect Backlash Toward Agentic Women," Psychology of Women Quarterly, Vol. 32, Issue 4, 2008 - https://journals.sagepub.com/doi/abs/10.1111/j.1471-6402.2008.00454.x?journalCode=pwqa

Prime, Jeanine L, Nancy M Carter and Theresa M Welbourne, "Women 'Take Care,' Men 'Take Charge': Managers' Stereotypic Perceptions of Women and Men Leaders," Psychologist-Manager Journal, Vol. 11, No. 2, August 2008, pp. 1-44 - http://cbafiles.unl.edu/public/cbainternal/facStaffUploads/women%20take%20care.2009.published.pdf

Reaves, Rhonda "Retaliatory Harassment: Sex and the Hostile Coworker as the Enforcer of Workplace Norms," Florida A&M University College of Law, Summer 2007, p. 409 - https://commons.law.famu.edu/cgi/viewcontent.cgi?referer=https://www.google.com/&httpsredir=1&article=1046&context=faculty-research

RMIT University, "Fact check: Are young Indigenous men more likely to end up in jail than university?" ABC News, 3 March 2016 - https://www.abc.net.au/news/2015-12-03/fact-check-aboriginal-men-in-jail-and-university/6907540

Rodrick, Stephen, "Serena Williams: The Great One," Rolling Stone, 18 June 2013 - https://www.rollingstone.com/culture/culture-sports/serena-williams-the-great-one-88694/

Ronson, Jon, So You've Been Publicly Shamed, Picador, 2015

Rosette, Ashleigh Shelby, Jennifer S Mueller and R David Lebel, "Are male leaders penalized for seeking help?" The Leadership Quarterly, 26, 2015, pp. 749–762 - https://klm68f.media.zestyio.com/shelby-rosette_mueller_lebel_2015-lq-leadership-and-asking-for-help.pdf

Rothenberg, Ben, "Tennis's Top Women Balance Body Image with Ambition," The New York Times, 10 July 2015 - https://www.nytimes.com/2015/07/11/sports/tennis/tenniss-top-women-balance-body-image-with-quest-for-success.html?smid=tw-nytimes&_r=2&referrer=

Rudman, Laurie A, Kris Mescher, and Cornnie A Moss-Racusin, "Reactions to gender egalitarian men: Perceived feminization due to stigma-by-association," Group Processes & Intergroup Relations, Vol.16, Issue 5, 2013, pp. 572–599 - https://journals.sagepub.com/doi/abs/10.1177/1368430212461160#articleCitationDownloadContainer

Russell, Brenda L and Debra Oswald, "When Sexism Cuts Both Ways: Predictors of Tolerance of Sexual Harassment of Men," Men and Masculinities, Vol. 19, Issue 5, 2015 - https://journals.sagepub.com/doi/full/10.1177/1097184X15602745

Safi, Michael, "AFL great Adam Goodes is being booed across Australia. How did it come to this?", The Guardian, 29 July 2015 - https://www.theguardian.com/sport/blog/2015/jul/29/afl-great-adam-goodes-is-being-booed-across-australia-how-did-it-come-to-this

Schechter, Danny, "Nelson Mandela's contested legacy," Al Jazeera, 16 July 2011 - https://www.aljazeera.com/indepth/opinion/2011/07/201172141053378510.html

Schmitt, David P, "The Truth About Sex Differences," Psychology Today, 7 November 2017 - https://www.psychologytoday.com/intl/articles/201711/the-truth-about-sex-differences

Seferian, Jacob, "Unpopular Opinion: Lady Gaga Shouldn't Win The Oscar," Wussy, 23 January 2019 - https://www.wussymag.com/all/2019/1/23/unpopular-opinion-lady-gaga-shouldnt-win-the-oscar

Semmelhack, Elizabeth in William Kremer, "Why did men stop wearing high heels?" BBC News, 25 January 2013 - https://www.bbc.com/news/magazine-21151350

Seth, Anil, "Your brain hallucinates your conscious reality," Ted Talk, Ted 2017, Vancouver, BC, 26 April 2017 - https://www.ted.com/talks/anil_seth_how_your_brain_hallucinates_your_conscious_reality?language=en

Shiv, Baba in Eilene Zimmerman, "Baba Shiv: Failure is the Mother of Innovation," Insights by Stanford Business, 2 March 2016 - https://www.gsb.stanford.edu/insights/baba-shiv-failure-mother-innovation

Shymansky, Nick in Kathryn Bromwich, "Amy Winehouse's manager Nick Shymansky: 'She'd be so sweet and funny, but there were warning signs...,'" The Guardian, 14 June 2015 - https://www.theguardian.com/music/2015/jun/14/amy-winehouse-manager-nick-shymansky-interview

Spencer, Charles, 9th Earl Spencer, "Earl Spencer's Funeral Oration," BBC, 6 September 1997 - http://www.bbc.co.uk/news/special/politics97/diana/spencerfull.html

Spicer, Tracey, "Keynote Speech," Calling out financial bias and imbalance, CEDA Women in Leadership Series, West Perth, 15 June 2017 (unpublished, transcript courtesy of Tracey Spicer)

Stables, Kate "Bohemian Rhapsody review: Freddie Mercury, tied up with a bow," BFI, UK, 26 February 2019 - https://www.bfi.org.uk/news-opinion/sight-sound-magazine/reviews-recommendations/bohemian-rhapsody-freddie-mercury-queen-biopic-trite-tidy

Stadlen, Matthew, "Maki Mandela: 'I'm very proud of my father - but he was not perfect or a saint," The Telegraph, UK, 14 October 2015 - https://www.telegraph.co.uk/news/worldnews/nelson-mandela/11931955/Maki-Mandela-Im-very-proud-of-my-father-but-he-was-not-perfect-or-a-saint.html

St James, James, "These 25 Examples of Male Privilege from a Trans Guy's Perspective Really Prove the Point," Everyday Feminism, 30 May 2015 - https://everydayfeminism.com/2015/05/male-privilege-trans-men/

Stone, Lucy, "The meeting that drove Netflix founders to bankrupt Blockbuster," Brisbane TImes, 8 July 2019 - https://www.brisbanetimes.com.au/national/queensland/the-meeting-that-drove-netflix-s-founders-to-bankrupt-blockbuster-20190708-p5255f.html

Summers, Anne, "Bill Shorten's biggest challenge is to make himself more likeable," The Sydney Morning Herald, 8 September 2017 - https://www.smh.com.au/opinion/bill-shortens-biggest-challenge-is-to-make-himself-more-likeable-20170908-gydbcl.html

Swift, Taylor, Max Martin and Shellback, Shake It Off, 1989, Big Machine Records, 2014

Tailor, Leena, "Fall Preview 2018: How Lady Gaga Conquered Music, Fashion and Film in Just a Decade," ET Online, 4 September 2018 - https://www.etonline.com/how-lady-gaga-conquered-music-fashion-and-film-fall-preview-106993

Taylor, Roger (and Brian May) with Mike Morris and Kathryn Holloway (interviewers), "Roger Taylor and Brian May Interview One Week After Freddie Mercury Death," TV-AM, ITV, December 1991, published on YouTube, 13 February 2019 - https://www.youtube.com/watch?v=XC2RfXMkrT0

Van Ness, Jonathan, @jvn, Twitter, 26 August 2019 - https://twitter.com/jvn/status/1166168929103962117

Waxman, Olivia, "The U.S. had Nelson Mandela on Terrorist Watch Lists Until 2008. Here's Why," TIME, 18 July 2018 - https://time.com/5338569/nelson-mandela-terror-list/

Winehouse, Amy in "Amy Winehouse Unpublished Interview From 2004 - 'I Never Want To Remember Anything Bad In My Life,'" The Huffington Post, UK, 18 July 2014 - https://www..huffingtonpost.co.uk/2014/07/18/amy-winehouse-unpublished-interview-2004_n_5598705.html

Zaidi, Tariq, "There's no Tinder in the desert: How Chad's Wodaabe nomads find love," Adventure.com, 27 August 2018 - https://adventure.com/wodaabe-nomads-gerewol-chad-africa/

Zoladz, Lindsay, "Lady Gaga goes to the middle," Vulture, New York Magazine, 13 July 2015 - https://www.vulture.com/2015/07/lady-gaga-goes-normal.html

www.ingramcontent.com/pod-product-compliance
Lightning Source LLC
Chambersburg PA
CBHW032039290426
44110CB00012B/877